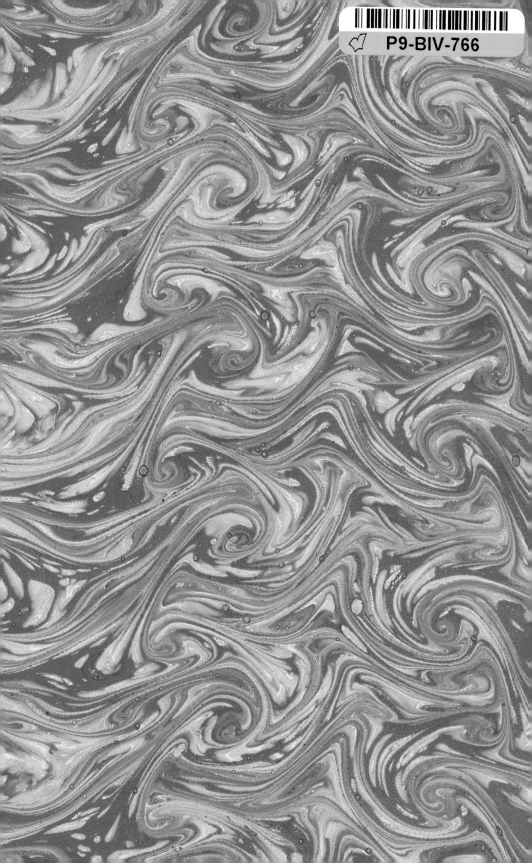

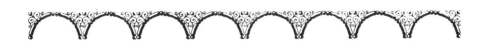

KAPELLMEISTER HUMMEL
IN
ENGLAND AND FRANCE

Joel Sachs

Detroit Monographs in Musicology Number Six
Information Coordinators
Detroit
1977

To Gail and Erica

Contents

Preface

JOHANN NEPOMUK HUMMEL is a classic example of an artist enormously successful and revered in his lifetime but consigned by posterity to its more thorough history books. Although he enjoyed a reputation as Europe's greatest pianist and improvisor, and a place as a composer second only to Beethoven, Hummel is now remembered only as the composer of a few concertos and chamber works. Yet while Hummel was certainly not one of the true giants, his career was so successful that it yields important insights into the everyday musical life of the early nineteenth century.

Hummel's international touring is perhaps the most fascinating aspect of his career because of the many cultures it spanned and the changing audiences that it reached. Like his teacher Mozart—in fact, at Mozart's suggestion—he commenced his international career hardly a step away from the cradle: at the age of ten he set out on a tour of continental Europe and Britain that lasted five years. Apparently this temporarily satisfied his urge to perform, for after leaving England (cancelling a trip to France because of revolutionary turmoil), he settled down in Vienna for a decade of study, teaching, and composing, followed by a period of employment with the Esterházy family in Eisenstadt, and then more free-lance work in Vienna. When the glitter of the Congress of Vienna (1814-1815) finally prompted him to return to the stage, his real activities as a pianist began. From that time until the early 1830's, almost every year saw a concert tour, often of major proportions.

As he now had a wife and two children, he realized the desirability of a job that would combine stability with adequate free time for touring. After an aggravating year in Stuttgart, Hummel, in 1818, found such a post as Kapellmeister in Weimar. In this position he had responsibility for music in concerts, theater, and at court, and frequently provided music for his Masonic lodge. Furthermore, he was increasingly sought after as a teacher. But above all, business in England and France dominated his activities. To begin with, these countries stimulated most of Hummel's public performances in the last decade of his life. Whereas in the early 1820's he travelled through most of Europe, from the Low Countries to Russia, his major tours after 1825 involved primarily England and France. His other tours during that period, only four in all, were confined to a short distance from home: in 1826, Berlin, Leipzig, and Dresden; in 1827, Vienna, to see the dying Beethoven; in 1828, Berlin, Warsaw, and Breslau; and in 1834, Vienna and Dresden. As the 1834 tour was Hummel's only one east of the Rhine in the last nine years of his life,[1] it is hardly surprising that the *Neue Zeitschrift für Musik's* obituary[2] described his pianistic control as "all the more astounding because of the rarity of his performances." Yet actually it was only on the Continent that his appearances were so infrequent.

England and France were also decisive influences on Hummel's compositional output for the twenty-odd years between his arrival at Weimar until his death there in 1837.[3] From England there was a steady flow of commissions for new works and arrangements; and many of his later works were composed for the French and English tours. The force of England and France was felt particularly strongly because Hummel was just then retreating from two areas of composition that had occupied much of his energy for years: occasional music and sacred music. The burden of composing occasional music—a responsibility that Hummel had carefully kept out of his contract at Weimar—diminished considerably after the death of Grand Duke Carl August in 1828. Furthermore, as a Catholic at the Protestant Weimar court, Hummel, right from the beginning, had been relieved of the duty of composing for church. With so few daily responsibilities for compositions, it seems therefore that the main impetus for new composing came from commissions or the needs of touring, both of which, it happened, largely involved England and France. Hummel was also one of the earliest to publish his compositions internationally and helped to lead the struggle for uniform copyright laws in Germany and Austria. This important aspect of his international life has been treated elsewhere, however, and need not be recapitulated here.[4]

The following study[5] deals with Hummel's trips to England and France during the Weimar Kapellmeister years.[6] It will not treat his tour as a prodigy, for such

---

[1] *Die neue Zeitschrift für Musik* communicated an erroneous report that Hummel was in Brussels in January, 1836. (January 15, 1836; corrected January 26.) The report was repeated (but not corrected) in *La Revue et Gazette Musicale*, January 24.

[2] *Die neue Zeitschrift für Musik,* November 17, 1837.

[3] See the list of Hummel's compositions of the Weimar period, Appendix. He provided much more occasional music than the Appendix suggests, but the other occasional works were from earlier days.

[4] On Hummel's various publishing activities see this author's "Hummel and George Thomson of Edinburgh," *Musical Quarterly*, LVI/2 (April, 1970), 270-287; "Authentic English and French Editions of J. N. Hummel," *Journal of the American Musicological Society*, XXV/2 (1972), 203-229; "Hummel and the Pirates: The Struggle for Musical Copyright," *Musical Quarterly*, LIX/1 (January, 1973), 31-60.

[5] This study results from research sponsored by a grant from the Foreign Area Fellowship Program, and was completed with the assistance of grants from the Columbia University Council for Research in the Humanities, the American Council of Learned Societies, and the National Endowment for the Humanities.

[6] Hummel's activities in England and France were touched on lightly in Karl Benyovszky, *J.N. Hummel: der Mensch und Künstler* (Bratislava: Eos, 1934).

tours involve criteria quite different from those governing the work of a long-established artist of great renown. Although outwardly biographical, this saga can also serve as an introduction to the international musical world of Hummel's Europe, to the methodology of creating and sustaining an international career in the early nineteenth century, and to the problems of assessing that career a century and a half later. For such an introduction, Hummel easily plays the leading role of the successful touring performer-composer. He was at the center of the European musical world, with a fame that could fill concert halls and earn him a substantial fortune. As a result, he dealt with the run of problems concerning the major artist, was widely discussed in the press, and left behind him a quantity of material that could only delight a historian.

In the course of writing this book, I found the wealth and style of journalistic and epistolary sources so captivating that I decided to tell as much of the story as possible through the words of the period, including their habit of referring to people by the surname alone. (Given names and a few marks of identification will be found in the index.) This presented the problem of an embarrassment of riches, since the volume of available material increased substantially during the era that the book encompasses. In France, information about concerts suddenly became abundant in 1827 with the founding of *La Revue Musicale*; in England, journals came and went, but the absolute number of words shed at any time seems to have swollen continually. If, as a consequence of my enjoyment of our ancestors' verbosity, I have erred on the side of excessive detail, I can only ask the reader's indulgence.[7]

---

[7] For the originals of the texts, see Joel Sachs, *Hummel in England and France: a Study in the International Musical Life of the Early Nineteenth Century* (diss., Columbia University, 1968). All translations are by the author.

Acknowledgements

THIS STUDY would not have been possible without the assistance of countless people throughout Europe. I am particularly indebted to Miss Maria Hummel, who, while making available all the material at her disposal concerning her great-grandfather, provided hospitality more than worthy of the traditions of her family and of Florence. Through the kindness of Dr. Karl Höhnel, director of the State Archive, Leipzig, who, with his staff devoted the better part of a sunny spring morning to a lightning search of uncatalogued material, I was able to consult the correspondence of the firms C. F. Peters and Breitkopf und Härtel. Other invaluable assistance was rendered by Dr. Iwan and Frau Kühn of the Landesbibliothek, Weimar; Mr. Oliver Neighbour and the music staff of The British Library; Mr. Swinyard of Novello and Co., London; Frau Dr. Theurich, of the German State Library, East Berlin; and Miss Ann Reardon, of the library of The London School of Economics. I wish also to extend my thanks to the staffs of the libraries and archives cited in this book, who, in all cases, helped my work to be smooth and efficient.

Library Sigla

Bds   Berlin, German State Library

Cu   Cambridge (England), University Library (manuscript division)

En   Edinburgh, National Library of Scotland

Lbm   London, British Library (formerly British Museum).
"Add." and "Loan" references are to the manuscript division

MH   Private collection of Maria Hummel, Florence

Pn   Paris, National Library

Wn   Vienna, Austrian National Library

WR   Weimar, Thuringian Provincial Library

WRa   Weimar, State Archive

The Paris Tour
1825

SHORTLY AFTER JOHANN NEPOMUK HUMMEL resumed his career as a public performer in the winter of 1814-1815, rumors began to circulate that he would make a trip to England, possibly with the great violinist Joseph Mayseder. The rumors seem to have had no basis, but their existence reminds us that a trip to England was a logical step for a man of great repute, particularly considering the Continental belief that the English stage was paved with gold. Indeed, an important invitation soon arrived—a summons, in 1821, from the elite Philharmonic Society of London, which, as we shall see in due course, came to nothing because of Hummel's busy schedule. Two years later, Friedrich Kalkbrenner, now living in London, urged Hummel to pay that musical world a visit, but commitments for other tours, duties at Weimar, and his desire to complete his *Piano Method* kept him from fulfilling Kalkbrenner's wish.[1]

Another reason for Hummel's failure to revisit England, which he had known and loved as a child some thirty years earlier, may have been his desire to see Paris. He had been deprived of a visit there at the end of his prodigy tour in 1793 because of the ill-timed French Revolution, and had yet to make a second attempt. Not long after the move to Weimar, however, we find hints that he was contemplating such a project. In the spring of 1821, while giving concerts in Berlin, Hummel must have mentioned a projected trip to France, for Spontini (Kapellmeister to the King of Prussia) wrote Hummel the following fall to ask about the state of the tour.[2] But in 1823 Hummel still had not gone there. Encouragement then came to him from the distinguished French violinist Pierre Rode: "Won't you ever come to France, where you will produce an enthusiasm which, in truth, you will produce all over, but which our nation can still show with more vivacity than others?"[3] A tour to Paris was, however, no simple matter. Competition would be ferocious in a capital that was always overflowing

---

[1] Kalkbrenner's letter: MH, printed Benyovszky pp. 311-12. The wish to see Hummel in London was never granted, thanks to a bigamy charge that precipitated Kalkbrenner's hasty departure. (See article "Kalkbrenner," *MGG*.)

[2] MH; printed Benyovszky, pp. 313-14.

[3] MH; printed Benyovszky, pp. 314-16. Dated Bordeaux, November 24, 1823.

LEFT: Johann Nepomuk Hummel. From *The Harmonicon*, London, June, 1824.

with what the English termed "the most admired musicians" of Europe. Further-more, in financial terms, the risks of so speculative a trip could be justified only if Hummel could remain there for some time.

His opportunity came in 1825. During the 1824 season he had relinquished his contractual three-month sabbatical in order to work on his *Piano Method*,[4] and petitioned the Grand Duke for permission to add that time to his next year's leave. His request was granted.[5] In the third week of February, armed with letters of introduction supplied by C. F. Peters, his friend and Leipzig publisher, Hummel left Weimar.[6] By the end of the month he was in Frankfurt. There, on Tuesday the 28th he gave a "grand instrumental and vocal concert," which was marked by the premature burning out of the lights, exactly as had happened at his previous concert a decade before![7] During this stay he met and accepted as a student Ferdinand Hiller, whose memoirs are an important source of information about Hummel's later years.[8] On Thursday he left Frankfurt for Paris, expecting to arrive Sunday evening.[9] The journey from Weimar to Paris would therefore have taken a tedious seven days. Luckily, he had the company of his elder son Eduard; his wife had stayed behind in Weimar with Karl, their second son.[10]

Despite Hummel's great fame, it is not easy to say what expectations the Parisians had of him before his arrival. Indeed, information of any sort is limited by the lack of a French musical periodical prior to the founding of *La Revue Musicale* (1827) and the sparse coverage of concerts in the local newspapers. There is even a further complication: subtle indications of corruption among the critics suggest that much of the available information ought to be disregarded. This is an unaffordable luxury, however, given the slender resources; a charitable approach is required. Seen in such a light, extant reports certainly establish that the colony of foreign musicians in Paris had already been very influential in introducing Hummel's music. Fétis wrote that Cherubini had been the first to bring Hummel's music from Vienna, playing the Fantasy for piano, Op. 18, at the

---

[4] Hummel had written to C. F. Peters on November 29, 1823, saying that instead of touring in 1824 he would stay at home to enjoy his house and complete the *Piano Method*. (Leipzig, State Archive; printed Benyovszky, p. 229.)

[5] WRa, A9866, f. 39.

[6] Letters to Peters, October 16, November 9, 1824; January 18, 1825: Leipzig, State Archive.

[7] Leipzig *Allg. mus. Zeitung*, April 27, 1825.

[8] Hiller (Frankfurt, 1811 - Cologne, 1885) was a well known pianist, composer, and conductor. On the advice of Spohr and Moscheles, he went to study with Hummel in Weimar. He was introduced to Viennese musical circles by Hummel in 1827, and to Parisian circles on his recommendations in 1828. In later life Hiller was a close associate of Liszt, Mendelssohn, and Wagner. His many volumes of memoirs contain much important information about Hummel's later years, particularly *Künstlerleben* (Cologne: Dumont-Schauberg, 1880).

[9] Letter to Tobias Haslinger, the Vienna publisher: Bds, Mus. ep. J. N. Hummel 7.

[10] Letters to Peters, October 16, 1824, January 18, 1825: Leipzig, State Archive.

Conservatory in 1806.[11] Henri Herz had played a set of variations by Hummel in Paris in 1817;[12] Liszt played the B-minor Concerto in 1824 [13] and another in 1825; [14] he had also performed the B-minor Concerto in Strasbourg in 1823.[15] Another important sign is the fact that by 1824 Hummel's music was being included in volumes awarded as prizes by the Conservatory.[16] (Here Cherubini may again have been responsible, since he was now director of the Conservatory.)

These bits of information obviously permit little more than vague inferences about what kind of reputation preceded Hummel to France. Nevertheless, the German-speaking Parisians anticipated his sojourn eagerly and provided bulletins for the home front. In the issue of March 16, 1825, the *Berliner allgemeine musikalische Zeitung* informed its readers, in a report from Paris:

> We expect Hummel in March . . . . The greatest German pianists are
> now assembled in Paris, or rather will be in a short time: Hummel,
> Moscheles, Kalkbrenner, Mayerbeer [*sic*], little Schauroth (a
> student of Kalkbrenner, a very lovely talent) and Mlle. Belleville;
> the French cannot produce a single one.

German pride, however, could not match Austrian admiration for their native son, and regular articles in the *Wiener Zeitschrift* and the *Allgemeiner musikalischer Anzeiger* (edited by Hummel's close friend Ignaz Castelli) kept them aware of the traveller's progress. Clearly the Viennese themselves were about to conquer Paris.

After Hummel arrived in Paris, his name began to appear very often in the Parisian newspapers. But caution! Any assessment of a virtuoso's visit to Paris must take into account an important fact of life: the popularity of an artist cannot be judged by the frequency with which his name is mentioned in Parisian

---

11 François-Joseph Fétis, *Biographie Universelle des Musiciens.* Fétis wrote that despite Hummel's fame in Germany and Austria, "his name was absolutely unknown in France when, in 1806, Cherubini brought from Vienna his Grand Fantasy (in E-flat, Op. 18), which was played at the Conservatory Competition the same year: this was the first work of Hummel that one heard in Paris. It was understood only by the artists; but this success sufficed to establish the reputation of the composer, and from that moment on his works were sought out by all pianists." (The article was written for the first edition of the *Biographie*, 1833-1844, and printed in *La Revue et Gazette Musicale,* August 8, 1839, pp. 292-93.)

12 Max Unger, *Muzio Clementis Leben* (diss., Leipzig, 1913), p. 207.

13 Leipzig *Allg. mus. Ztg.,* May 6, 1824. The correspondent wrote that the piano sank a half-step in one movement, causing the concert to be stopped while the instrument was tuned and the broken strings replaced.

14 *Wiener Zeitschrift für Kunst, Literatur, Theater, und Mode*, May 26, 1825.

15 Leipzig *Allg. mus. Ztg.,* September 23, 1824.

16 Copies; Pn, L3621 and Ac. p. 2266.

newspapers because many items posing as news may have actually been advertisements. In fact, what may have been the first word of Hummel's arrival in Paris—an announcement in *Le Journal des Débats* (March 21)—was one such mysterious "news item" that curiously resembles advertising. It is amusing to note that the publisher Maurice Schlesinger, who provided this publicity, was by no means a friend of Hummel: [17]

> The arrival at Paris of MM. Hummel and Moscheles could not fail to make one seek out with new avidity the piano compositions of these two musicians: thus the beautiful edition of their works published, on subscription, by MM. Schlesinger, dealers in music to the King, rue de Richelieu no. 97, is having a success that continually increases. The collection of the works of M. Hummel will form 21 volumes of 60 to 100 plates each, engraved by MM. Richomme and Marquerie, and printed on Annonay paper. The price of subscription, 7 francs. Eight volumes are on sale. That of the works of M. Moscheles will have 18 volumes, of which two are published. The price is likewise 7 francs for subscribers. The *dilettanti* are aware of the exactitude of the publishers of Mozart and Rossini. We cannot doubt that these two enterprises will be completed soon.

One is overwhelmed by the urge to assume that so large an edition indicates Schlesinger's high regard for Hummel's music. This is certainly correct; Schlesinger knew what would sell. Unfortunately for the holders of the rights to Hummel's works, the edition was a piracy.

Hummel's activities now commenced. According to the Leipzig *Allgemeine musikalische Zeitung*, Hummel gave a great number of private concerts in Paris, presumably in homes, but the discretion of Society has obliterated all details. For the public, the high point of his visit was a subscription series, four Friday soirées, at the salon of the piano makers and publishers Erard, rue du Mail, no. 13. Hardly had his series been announced (on March 23), however, when Hummel's name appeared in connection with another concert, a circumstance that was by no means to enhance his reputation. This event, scheduled for April 6, was to be given by a certain singer, Mme. Cornega, and the pianist Charles Schunke, who enticed the public with the ambiguous line, "M. Hummel will be at the piano." Alas, when *Le Journal des Débats* gave the full program on the day of the concert, ticket holders must have been dismayed to learn the meager extent of Hummel's participation: he would be heard only in the concluding work, Moscheles' arrangement for two pianos, eight hands, of the overture to Cherubini's opera *Les deux Journées*. (The other performers were Moscheles, Pixis, and Schunke.) Two facts are unclear: whether Hummel agreed to participate for money or out of deference to Cherubini, and why, to

---

[17] See Sachs, "Hummel and the Pirates," *op. cit.*

everyone's dismay, he backed out at the last moment. *La Gazette de France* (April 11) berated Schunke for not having advised the public of the change in cast although he surely had had enough notice of "Hummel's perhaps natural desire to save himself for his own concerts." Indeed, expecting the long-awaited pleasure of hearing Hummel, music lovers had flocked to the concert.

While Hummel was still embroiled in this mistaken venture, preparations got under way for his own series. Erard, whose sales of pianos would surely have profited from Hummel's endorsement, did far more than simply rent his concert hall to him—he provided the pianist with his finest instruments, full use of his facilities, and even an apartment in his own home.[18] But all of this was, naturally, preparatory for the central problem, attracting audiences. In this quest, nothing was left to chance. Major newspapers, which did not ordinarily carry extensive concert announcements, printed many "news items" about his series. One wonders who was responsible for their insertion—Erard, Hummel, or others. These bulletins, appearing a few days before each concert, or even on the same day, were carefully phrased to avoid seeming like advertisements and even omitted the subscription price. But they were crass enough to reveal the information that before the first concert, subscriptions (apparently costing forty francs)[19] and remaining single tickets would be available at Erard's, Pleyel's, and Schlesinger's music shops. (Hummel later placed tickets at Lemoine's and Richault's, and thereby completed a comprehensive list of distributors.)

By the standards of the time, Hummel's programs should have had broad public appeal. Their format was typical of the era:

APRIL 8, 8:00 P.M.

1. Concerto, [Op. 85], composed and played by Hummel.
2. Air, sung by Mlle. Schiasetti. Composer unidentified.
3. Solo for flute, composed and played by M. Tulou.
4. *Rondo brillant* [probably Op. 98], composed and played by Hummel.
5. Duet, unidentified, sung by Mlle. Schiasetti and M. Zucchelli.
6. Improvisation by Hummel.

APRIL 15, 8:00 P.M.

1. Quintette, [Op. 87], composed by Hummel, played by him with MM. Videil (violin), Sina (viola), Norblin (cello), Lami (double bass).
2. Air, unidentified, sung by Mme. Pasta.
3. Solo for French horn, composed and played by M. Dauprat.
4. *"Nouvelle sonate"* for piano and cello ("encore manuscrite"— published as Op. 104), played by Hummel and Norblin.
5. Duo, composed by Rossini, sung by Mme. Pasta and M. Pellegrini.
6. Improvisation by Hummel.

---

18 *Wiener Zeitschrfit* . . . , April 9, 1827.
19 Acc. *ibid.*, which gave as its source "a Parisian newspaper."

APRIL 22, 8:00 P.M.

1. Sonata, piano four-hands [Op. 92], composed by Hummel, played by Hummel and Kalkbrenner.
2. Air, unidentified, sung by Mme. Marconi-Schönberger.
3. Variations for mandolin, composed [?] and played by M. Vimercati.
4. Terzette by Paer, sung by Mlle. Dorus, Mme. Marconi-Schönberger, M. Levasseur.
5. Trio [Op. 83], composed by Hummel, played by him with MM. Baillot (violin), and Norblin (cello).
6. Air, unidentified, sung by Mlle. Dorus.
7. Improvisation by Hummel.

APRIL 29, 8:00 P.M.

1. Septet, Op. 74, by Hummel, with MM. Guillou (flute), Brod (oboe), Dauprat (horn), Urhan (viola), Norblin (cello), and Lami (double bass).
2. Air, unidentified, sung by Mlle. Cinti.
3. Sonata for piano and violin [Op. 108?], by Hummel, played by him and Lafont.
4. Variations for oboe by Hummel [Op. 102], played by Brod.
5. "Airs suisses, variés et executés par Lafont."
6. Quartet by Rossini, sung by Mlle. Cinti and MM. Bordogni, Levasseur, and Panseron.
7. Improvisation by Hummel. [20]

The elaborateness of these programs suggests extensive preparations before Hummel's arrival. Actually, little seems to have been done until the last moment. For example, the violinist Baillot agreed to play at the third concert only a week and a half before it took place. [21] Hummel wrote to the bass Levasseur on the 20th (Wednesday) asking him to rehearse the following day for the concert of the 22nd, enclosing the music (to a trio from Paer's *Sargino*) and assuring him that the rehearsal would consume no more than a quarter of an hour. [22] (This letter also indicates that for at least some of the vocal music, Hummel himself was the accompanist.) [23] Yet if the rehearsal time seems miniscule for a large Hummel Trio, it may not have necessarily produced the result that one might fearfully anticipate. Luckily, the traditional concept of chamber music with piano, in which the keyboard dominated, made it possible for such concerts to be assembled rapidly. In fact, this style of "Trio for pianoforte with accompaniment of . . . " may have persisted precisely because travelling virtuosi often had to cope

---

[20] The programs are from *La Gazette de Paris*, April 7, 15, 20, and 28, 1825. According to *La Gazette de France*, April 11, the Concerto on the first program was Op. 85.

[21] MH.

[22] Pn, W.40.B (270).

[23] An undated letter from Mme. Pasta (MH; printed Benyovszky p. 262) suggests that he may also have accompanied her at the second concert.

with restricted rehearsal time or inexperienced accompanists. In this respect Hummel was lucky to have Baillot and Norblin, both first-rate musicians who had frequently collaborated. Furthermore, Mlle. Schiasetti had sung in Hummel's Munich concert, 1820; Mme. Marconi-Schönberger probably knew him from years back in Vienna.

Even with limited rehearsals, the expenses of the series must have been formidable. To begin with, Hummel had to hire enough supporting artists to create the crowd-drawing effect of a spectacle. Moreover, free tickets were distributed to an indeterminable number of notables.[24] All things considered, the private appearances, rather than the subscription series, may have proved the most profitable for the visiting musician. It was these events that brought Hummel into close contact with his admirers, and particularly with wealthy patrons. Perhaps it was at such an evening that Hummel met Caroline, Duchess of Berry, who became one of his important French sponsors.[25]

The private parties were so private that we cannot even guess at their effect. In a sense we are in not much better a position when trying to evaluate the subscription series. Anyone who has ever attended concerts and read the reviews has frequently observed the lack of agreement between the event and the report thereof. How much more so must it have been in Hummel's Paris, whose journalists were said to keep their palms permanently outstretched. We must therefore conclude from reviews of his series that Hummel had either enormous success or ample friends with connections at the newspapers. If we are again charitable, however, we learn that here, as all over Europe, Hummel's audiences were most impressed by his improvising, and, as elsewhere, his compositions were praised as "learned" and tasteful.

While we must remain cautious in interpreting the reviews, Hummel's success is also strongly suggested by his decision to give a fifth concert. Originally scheduled for May 15, this concert initially had to be postponed because it conflicted with Pentecost and festival days celebrating the return of the King to Paris.[26] Hummel was, however, not one to lose precious time. While the date of his farewell concert was still being decided, he appeared in a program given May 20 by the soprano Mlle. Dorus, who had sung in Hummel's third subscription concert. Happily, this time his participation was slightly more substantial than that scheduled for Schunke's ill-fated evening the previous month: Hummel played one of his *Rondeaux brillants* with orchestra.

---

[24] *E.g.*, to Boieldieu, who unfortunately could not use it. (MH; printed Benyovszky pp. 262-63.)

[25] *Journal des Débats*, April 17, 1825. The Duchess, daughter-in-law of Charles X and daughter of Francis I of Naples, was described in the Berlin *Allg. mus. Ztg.* (March 27, 1830) as "the only one in the Royal family who has a sense for good music." Hummel wrote the "Amusement" Op. 108 (a violin-piano Sonatina) for her.

[26] Pn, envelope of Hummel letters, No. 10; dated May 10, 1825, and addressed to the Count of Chabrol.

The farewell concert finally took place May 23, in the auditorium of the Conservatory, the "Salle des Menus-Plaisirs," at 2:00. For this concert, ticket prices were reduced to ten, eight, and six francs, possibly in response to complaints about the high price of the subscription series.[27] The program was, according to *La Gazette de Paris* (May 19),

1. Overture by Hummel.
2. Les Adieux, nouveau concerto, "composé et executé pour la première fois à Paris" by Hummel.
3. Air, unidentified, sung by Mlle. Cinti.
4. Concerto by Kalkbrenner, arranged for harp and played by Mlle. Céleste Boucher.
5. Duo, unidentified, sung by Mlle. Cinti and M. Zucchelli.
6. *Rondo brillant* in B flat [Op. 98], composed and played by Hummel.
7. Quartet by Cherubini (from *L'Hôtellerie portugaise*), sung by Mlle. Cinti, MM. Donzelli, Zucchelli, and Levasseur.
8. Variations for violin, composed and played by M. Baillot.
9. Improvisation by Hummel.

As in the case of the subscription series, program information is scanty, and only a few miscellaneous facts survive to illuminate the event. For the most part, these concern the orchestra, which was that of the conservatory, and was conducted by François Antoine Habaneck *l'aîné*. (The vocal quartet was performed only with piano accompaniment, played by Hummel himself.) While one of the odd features of all these concerts is the scarcity of new works by Hummel, the performance of *Les Adieux* was its first in Paris. But it had not been specifically composed for the Parisians, as they had been misled into believing; the autograph is dated 1814, and Hummel had performed it at least as early as 1816.[28] He had probably felt the need for a novelty at his final concert—the Cello Sonata was so far the only unpublished piece he had offered[29]—and palmed off the old Concerto as the latest product of his pen. This ruse seems to have succeeded, for the following summer a German journalist claimed (in the *Berliner allgemeine musikalische Zeitung*, July 12, 1826) that it had been written as a compliment to the Paris public. And Hummel actually allowed it to retain its Parisian identity: when it was finally published, as Op. 110, it bore a dedication to the Conservatory, whose director was still Hummel's old friend Cherubini.[30] Since such dedications were often tokens of gratitude, it may

---

[27] Program and prices from *La Gazette de Paris*, May 19, 1825; other information from *La Gazette de France*, May 25, 1825.

[28] Leipzig, *Allg. mus, Ztg.*, May 22, 1816.

[29] The Sonata for violin and piano on the fourth concert must not have been Op. 108, which certainly would have been promoted as a new work.

[30] Further on Hummel saving this Concerto for just such an occasion, see Sachs, "Hummel and the Pirates," *op. cit.* Hummel's ties with Cherubini were maintained, and Hummel was able to return a favor by presenting Cherubini's music to the Grand Duchess of Saxe-Weimar. See Benyovszky, pp. 264-71.

have resulted from some favor done for Hummel by Cherubini, such as arranging for Hummel to use the Conservatory auditorium and orchestra free of charge.

Although the programs of the five concerts lacked more than a smattering of new music, they abounded in variety. The public heard its favorite singers, vocal music by local composers, and music for many different soloists and ensembles. But programming was certainly governed by more than mere musical considerations. In one instance—the Kalkbrenner Piano Concerto arranged for harp—a place on the program was offered to right a wrong Hummel feared he had done to the husband of the harpist.[31]

Was the Paris trip an overall success? By inference from the large number of concerts, combined with the vague but consistent newspaper references to the "numerous and brilliant society" present, the answer is most certainly yes. Let us hope that *La Gazette de France* expressed generally-held sentiments in its review (May 25) of the farewell concert. The newspaper began by reminding the Parisians of their habit of exalting foreigners on the one hand, and showing extreme jealousy of them on the other. Nevertheless,

> Within this general disposition of temperaments, let a foreigner, an artist celebrated in all of Europe, present himself, joining to the superiority of his talent and his reputation a simple exterior, a sweet and modest physiognomy, certainly one seeks out such a rare man, one exalts him, one extols him to the skies. And who would reproach such a laudable and natural eagerness: who would want to restrict the extent of the eulogies and moderate the enthusiasm of the applause? These eulogies, this applause, are a pure homage that we render to genius.
>
> The celebrated artist of whom we have just sketched some characteristics is not an ideal figure without an embodiment: all lovers of music will recognize him in the person of M. Hummel, who, for two months, has charmed us at our concerts, and who just addressed to the public the most tender and harmonious *adieux* in a last afternoon concert, to which the best Parisian society and many of the learned, the artists, and the men of letters were eager to flock.

The reviewer ended by expressing his desire to see Hummel in Paris once more, and was inclined to believe that a return visit would bring a new work destined for the grand opera. He was inclining, as we shall see shortly, in the correct direction.

---

31 Letter to M. Boucher, May 4, 1825 (Pn. W.2 [55]). (Mlle. Boucher was actually Mme.) Unfortunately, only two isolated details are known about Hummel's conduct with the other guest artists. According to *La Gazette de France* (April 25), Kalkbrenner had the honor of playing "top" in the four-hands Sonata. Urhan and Lamis received a total of sixty-five francs for their participation in the performance of the Septet at the fourth concert, but Norblin requested for himself only "some measures for the Pianoforte written by your hands" in his album, as the best souvenir of Hummel's visit. (Letter from Norblin: May 25, 1825; original, MH.) Although he did not take part in the concerts, Hummel's old friend Moscheles also requested something for his album. (See Benyovszky, p. 263.)

The success of Hummel's tour also reached the "outside world" and provided the pianist with good publicity. London's *Quarterly Musical Magazine and Review* (VII, 313) translated from an unidentified German periodical an article entitled "Assemblage of piano-forte players in Paris in the Spring of 1825," which concluded,

> By speaking of the celebrated Hummel last, we wish to reserve a special place for treating of one who justly stands in the first rank of his profession. When this admirable artist took the resolution of visiting Paris, where his compositions have long been known and appreciated, the curiosity of the public was highly excited. It was expected that there would be found in his execution not only the highest degree of brilliancy, but the very excess of those difficulties which modern style so much affects. These expectations, however, were very ill founded. Chasteness, moderation, and gracefulness, are his distinguishing characteristics, and instead of charlatanism were found science and power; the delight and admiration of the audience were succeeded by astonishment; for such are the deep resources of his art, that they appear inexhaustible. His extemporaneous playing, which is of the very highest order of excellence, produced the greatest enthusiasm in his hearers. Of the many exquisite regular compositions which he performed we shall only mention his beautiful 7th [septet], which was received with reiterated applause, and which excited a universal desire to hear it again. He gave four soirèes (*sic*) in the house of Mr. Erard, of which the two last, notwithstanding the unusually high price of twelve francs per ticket,[32] attracted very numerous and select audiences. This was also the case in the concert which he afterwards gave in the Salle des Menus Plaisirs, or Music Saloon of the Royal Conservatory.
> To prove how highly they esteemed his extraordinary talents, the artists and amateurs had a medal struck by subscription. On one side is a bust of the artist, and on the other the following inscription: 'Les artistes et Amateurs François à Hummel, 1825.' A book containing all the subscribers' names, was presented to him at the same time with the medal.

The Harmonicon (June, 1825) printed a similarly ecstatic report (probably by its own correspondent) containing only one reservation:

> The sonata for two performers, executed by Kalkbrenner and Hummel, appeared learned and original. An adagio in the old style, if it had lasted much longer would have fatigued the auditory. Interminable cadences, and shakes a quarter of an hour long, may prove the skill of the performer . . . but these ornaments of the old school, to be at all bearable, should be short.

---

[32] If this report is accurate, the price of twelve francs must have been to non-subscribers. Expensive tickets for Paris concerts ordinarily cost ten francs.

Alas, these comments would in the end prove fatal: the association of Hummel with archaism, the style of Mozart, and excessive "learnedness," were strong factors in the eventual decline of his reputation as a composer and pianist. This was still in the future, however, for the fruits of these three months in Paris were considerable. The Leipzig *Allgemeine musikalische Zeitung* (September 7) hinted at substantial profit in summarizing the trip by saying, "The public was fully contented with Hummel's performances, and he had reason as well to be satisfied with the public." The trip also yielded arrangements for future publication of his new works by Farrenc and Erard, and the dubious distinction of *two* large piracies: the collected edition published by Schlesinger (mentioned earlier), and a collection of his piano music issued on subscription by Richault. These editions would have exercised a detrimental financial effect on Hummel's German publishers, had not the majority of the major works already appeared at least once in French pirated editions.

The tour also produced some other honors, such as George Onslow's dedication of a new work to Hummel in 1826, but a distinction that was much more useful for keeping his memory alive was Hummel's election to the *Société Académique des Enfans d'Apollon*, a Parisian organization, founded in 1741, with members of both sexes, from all artistic fields and all countries. The various "arts" held their own monthly meetings, and on Ascension Day all members would assemble for a general session—open to the public—comprising a concert, a speech, and a banquet. In 1825, this concert occurred during Hummel's tour and included his Gradual *Quod quod in orbe*; the speech mentioned compositions of Hummel and Moscheles.[33] His election may well have been announced on this occasion, although he did not receive the official certificate until December.[34] During the subsequent two decades, Hummel's music became a regular part of the Society's concerts. As we shall see, he improvised twice at the closed session in March, 1830; his B-minor Piano Concerto was selected for the grand hundredth anniversary concert in 1841.[35] There was an even greater honor in store for Hummel, however—election as a *Chevalier* of the Legion of Honor. The certificate (signed by the King) is dated November 3, 1826, and the new title soon found its way into Hummel's formal signature.[36]

The most significant musical result of the trip was a commission for an opera, alluded to above and revealed in *The Harmonicon*, March, 1826:

---

[33] Maurice Decourcelle, *La Société Académique des Enfants d'Apollon* (1741-1880), (Paris: Durand, Schoenewerk, 1881), pp. 60,138. Liszt, then 14 years old, played music by Czerny and improvised on that same program. The records for the closed sessions of 1825 are missing.

[34] The certificate: MH.

[35] Decourcelle, p. 142; Leipzig *Allg. mus. Ztg.*, July 7, 1841. The other works on the anniversary program were a Haydn Symphony and a Viotti Violin Concerto.

[36] The certificate: MH.

> By a private letter from Weimar, dated the 27th of January last,
> we learn that the celebrated J. N. Hummel . . . is engaged to write
> an Opera for the *Grand Opéra* of Paris, and is at present exclusively
> employed in fulfilling that engagement.

The work was to be called *Attila*, and was based on a new libretto by Victor
Joseph Étienne de Jouy. According to *La Revue Musicale* (May, 1827), it was
one of a number of commissions stemming from a decision by the newly-
reorganized opera administration to enlarge the traditionally miniscule repertoire
of the company. Since Hummel had had years of experience composing for the
Esterházy and Viennese stages—some fourteen dramatic works, three ballets, and
two pantomimes—it was not unnatural that they looked to him. At the time of
La Revue Musicale's report, eighteen of the commissions had already been
completed. The journal listed still six works as being in progress:

	LIBRETTO	MUSIC
Le Vieux de la Montagne	Jouy	Rossini
Attila	Jouy	Hummel
Érostrate	Halévy	Halévy
Sardanapale	Viennet	Schneitzhöffer
Les Athéniennes	Jouy	Spontini
Le Duc de Clarence	Scribe	Kalkbrenner

It was an impressive group, but the article expressed the fear that not even the
prestige of the composers would prevent the lethargic Opéra management from
leaving the works unperformed.

In Hummel's case the problem was more basic. Despite the promising
newspaper reports, *Attila* progressed none too smoothly. Hummel's habit of not
answering letters disconcerted the librettist, who wrote from Paris, January 8, 1826:

> My dear collaborator,
>
> It is now at least six weeks since I sent you, by the Paris-Weimar
> stagecoach, adorned with all the customs formalities, the manuscript
> of *The Amazon and Lutèce*: the roll was stamped; on the same day
> I had franked at the post office a letter which informed you of the
> shipment and asked you to notify me of its arrival.
> I told you, among other things, that our opera [*i.e.* the libretto]
> had produced the greatest effect both in the private readings and
> before the jury, which received it unanimously.
> Since that time the Viscount de la Rochefoucault, who knows that
> you are to compose the music for this opera, has written me to testify
> to his desire to see it staged as soon as possible, regarding the receipt
> of this work as a truly happy occasion for the *Académie royale de
> Musique* [the Opera].

I shall receive this assurance with the greatest pleasure and I beg you to keep me frequently informed of the progressive march of our work so that I can inform the Director of Fine Arts about it . . . .[37]

Jouy's fears that the earlier letter had gone astray were unfounded—it still survives in the Hummel collection in Florence. What Jouy *should* have worried about was the completion of the opera. For although Hummel had begun with enthusiasm[38] he soon faltered. In a letter of October 18, 1828, he requested that his student Ferdinand Hiller—who was then taking up residence in Paris—parry any inquiries about the opera with the excuse that it was being delayed because of Hummel's poor health and extra duties resulting from changes in the Weimar Theater administration after the recent death of Grand Duke Carl August. The truth was that Hummel simply wanted no discrepancies between Hiller's response and that which he had already written to Jouy. He advised Hiller, "these days one doesn't always have to tell people the real reason . . ."[39]

Many years later Hiller described the fate of the opera in his memoirs:

> In Paris [Hummel] had been given a French libretto, which he undertook to compose for the Grand Opera. Whether it was the text or the substance (I think that the hero was Attila) that spoiled his desire for it—it was forgotten. But the greatest part of the first act must be among his posthumous sketches. As soon as he had completed a number he played and sang it to me, to my proudest joy. The pieces seemed most splendid to me; in particular I recall a truly original march, which charmed me. Frau Hummel was very annoyed that her husband threw away the opportunity to consort with the Parisian opera composers. That did not make him waver, however, and he sent back the libretto and the contract.[40]

The remains of this opera, Hummel's only major compositional endeavor for three years after the Paris tour, have now completely disappeared. It may be, in fact, that the project was, as a whole, ill-fated, for of all the others on *La Revue Musicale*'s list, only Schneitzhöffer's was even partly composed.

---

[37] MH. "De la Rochefoucault" was Ambroise-Polycarpe de la Rochefoucauld, Duc de Doudeauville. As Minister of the Royal Household, he was responsible for fine arts in France.
[38] He wrote to C. F. Peters, December 20, 1826, that he was working *only* on the opera. (Lbm, Add. 29,999, ff. 18-19; Benyovszky, pp. 304-306, with wrong date.)
[39] Benyovszky, pp. 217-18.
[40] *Künstlerleben*, p. 6.

The Tour of 1830
Paris and London

IN 1828, with his *Piano Method* at last complete, Hummel began once again to think about tours. Indeed, Fate must have been acting on behalf of the international concert-goer, for despite the element of deception in Hummel's communication to Hiller, the death of the Grand Duke that year actually had plunged the Weimar Theatre administration into such turmoil that Hummel had to cancel most of his contractual sabbatical for the spring of 1829. Since there was a precedent for adding unused vacation time to that of the following year, he could justifiably lay claim to a full six months' leave for 1830. Half a year was ideal for a truly grandiose project, so in March, 1829, he solicited the permission of the new Grand Duke, Carl Friedrich, to leave Weimar from February 20 (shortly after the ruler's birthday) until the end of July in order to visit England.[1] Although no reply from the Grand Duke survives, approval was obviously given. Hummel's correspondence does not indicate that he made any arrangements for the tour during the next months, but in a letter to George Thomson in Edinburgh, dated October 15, 1829, he mentioned a plan to go to England and the wish to return to Scotland, which he had visited as a prodigy in the 1790's.[2] Then, writing to Ferdinand Hiller in Paris, November 4, 1829, he revealed that another stop had been added: a fortnight in the French capital.[3]

The first step was to enlist some help with general preparations. Of particular interest is one sentence in his letter to Hiller: "Also I want *really a lot* said about my visit in advance, in the most eminent Parisian journals, from New Year's on, that I shall journey to London via Paris, *&c. &c.*—see to it that this is arranged...." The faithful Hiller must have gone into action immediately, for in its issue of late November, 1829, *La Revue Musicale* announced, "The celebrated pianist Hummel will arrive in Paris in the month of March, and from here move on to London, where he will spend the season." It was a well-planned press release. Because English editors regularly picked the bones of Continental periodicals—and especially this one—for second-hand news, Hummel's publicity apparatus in

---

[1] WRa, A9866, ff. 68-68¹. Printed Benyovszky, pp. 274-75.

[2] See Joel Sachs, "Hummel and George Thomson of Edinburgh. *op. cit.*

[3] Printed Benyovszky, p. 219.

London would be off to an early start. Indeed, London heard the news in the January edition of *The Monthly Musical and Literary Magazine*, along with a report that Paganini was expected there and in Paris. As usual, the news also reached the German-speaking world shortly. The Leipzig *Allgemeine musikalische Zeitung*'s correspondent proclaimed (February 3, 1830) that Hummel's memory was held in great esteem in Paris, although two weeks later, with no offense intended the French, the newspaper emphasized that London was the real goal of the tour. The Viennese *Allegmeiner musiklischer Anzeiger* (March 27) added the additional detail that Hummel would present a new Concerto and a Septet "that is supposed to be something extraordinary." Last, but hardly least, was London's *The Harmonicon*, which, by withholding its announcement until the issue for April (*i.e.* about April 1), gave the fickle London public a reminder only a week and a half before Hummel's expected arrival.

The more publicity, the better. Because of the visit to London, the speculative nature of this trip was even more pronounced than that of the earlier tour to Paris alone. To complicate matters, success in isolated England was rumored to be governed far less by ability than by connections and a good advance reputation. Some even considered those aids less important than careful attention to the well-being of the critics. Yet Hummel must have been confident. He knew that London, although distant from Germany, was culturally close to Paris. The sojourns in France would therefore do much to prepare the way for a triumphant return to England after forty years' absence.

A well-planned visit to Paris was therefore doubly important, and the omens were good. To begin with, Hummel's music had been performed there frequently during the five years since his last tour. Furthermore, information and discussions of these performances, his newer works, and his general activities, was widely disseminated thanks to *La Revue Musicale* (which also gives us a fuller picture of the Parisian musical world after 1827). Certainly, much of this local attention to Hummel is still attributable to the foreigners in Paris. Often they were prodigies, for whom the mastery of Hummel's music was considered a crucial milestone. The 1828 season contains several examples, of which the most important were two performances by the sixteen-year old Liszt. The first, of the Rondo of the B-minor Concerto at a Concert Spirituel, April 4, unfortunately had a mixed reception: *La Revue Musicale* (April) found the movement lacking in "chant" and disapproved of Liszt's use of "tricks" to astonish his audience. (This occasion also demonstrates how far-reaching such an event might be, for the review was repeated by *The Harmonicon* in June.) Liszt, however, was undeterred by the criticism of Hummel and himself, and presented Hummel's Septet Op. 74 on April 5, at his concert in the Salle Chantereine, this time with greater success. Rival prodigies also knew the value of a touch of Hummel: the Viennese brothers Leonard and Eduard Schulz, respectively a thirteen-year old guitarist and fifteen-year old pianist, gave a concert that same season which included a Concerto jointly written a decade earlier by Hummel and Mauro Giuliani, a guitar virtuoso then living in Vienna.[4]

Performances of Hummel's music were not restricted to the provenance of foreigners or prodigies, however, and certainly not to a few standard works. For example, when, in 1827, Alexandre-Étienne Choron's new Royal Institute of Religious Music announced six concerts (at the very low subscription price of twenty-five francs), the major sacred works scheduled were a Hummel Mass and compositions by Haydn (*Seven Last Words*), Palestrina (various compositions), Neukomm (a cantata), and Mozart (*Davidde Penitente* [K. 469]). The next year, Baillot included a Hummel String Quartet (wrongly called "new"—it was some twenty-five years old) in his chamber music concert.

As a consequence of these and other performances by foreigners and natives, the Parisian music lover had available a sampling of Hummel's work in different styles, and should have been well acquainted with his work as a pianist and teacher. Fétis, writing (in *La Revue Musicale*, May, 1827) on the state of music in Germany, summarized the French view of Hummel while lumping him together with some rather improbable compatriots:

> Among the pianists, Hummel, Moscheles, Ries, Pixis, and Czerny,
> have founded a new school, which, if it is no longer pure, is at least
> really brilliant, and several among them are first rate.

Paris Revisited

Hummel returned to Paris on March 5 and was welcomed by the local press with the hope "that he will give some concerts." One must not be misled by their coyness to infer that arrangements still had not commenced; Hiller as we know, had his instructions, and was both loyal and efficient. In addition, since his last trip to Paris, Hummel had maintained contact—personally or through Hiller—with many people who were doubtless of advance assistance. Among them were the Erards, Cherubini, and his good friend Zima (Mme. Adolphe) de Lanneau, a wealthy amateur pianist to whom Hummel dedicated two works.[5]

On March 13 *La Revue Musicale* finally had something more concrete to announce:

> M. Hummel arrived in Paris on the 6th. He is staying at the Hôtel des
> Princes, rue de Richelieu. This great artist, before betaking himself to
> London shortly, will only make a brief sojourn among us. We learn
> nevertheless that on the 22nd of March he will give a concert in the

---

[4] This lost and unverifiable Concerto was probably composed *ca.* 1815, when Giuliani and Hummel collaborated in outdoor concerts. The Schulzes had played Hummel's music in Vienna when only 8 and 10 years old.

[5] Mme. de Lanneau's husband was a noted educator, director of the School for Deaf Mutes, and *Maire* of Paris' 12th *Arrondissement* in the 1840's.

auditorium in the rue Chantereine. There he will improvise and
perform some unpublished works, among others a new concerto,
which is said to be really remarkable.

Hummel's triumphant return was now only two weeks away. His program's
contents (and a change of date) were announced (advertised?) in the *Courrier
des Théâtres* (March 19):

> At the auditorium in the rue Chantereine, no. 19, there will
> be a musical evening, instrumental and vocal, given by
> M. J.N. Hummel, Chapel-Master to the Court of Saxe-Weimar,
> before his departure for London, Wednesday the 24th of this
> month, at 8 o'clock in the evening precisely, instead of Monday,
> the 22nd. Here is the program: FIRST PART: 1. Overture.
> 2. Grand Concerto for piano, in A flat (unpublished), composed
> and executed by M. Hummel; 3. Air, sung by M.———;
> 4. Air varié for the flute, composed and executed by M. Camus.
> SECOND PART: 5. Air, sung by Mme.———; 6. Grand
> characteristic fantasy for the piano, with the accompaniment of
> orchestra (unpublished), composed and executed by M. Hummel;
> 7. Duo, sung by M.——— and Mme.———; 8. Improvisation
> on the piano, by M. Hummel. Price of seats: boxes, 12 fr.;
> orchestra stalls, 10 fr.; pit, 8 fr. For reservation of boxes, make
> application to M. Hummel, rue de Richelieu, Hôtel des Princes.
> The tickets for stalls and pit can be found at MM. J. Pleyel and
> Co., boulevart Montmartre; Pacini, boulevart des Italiens, no. 11;
> Schlesinger, rue de Richelieu, no. 97; Henri Lemoine, rue de
> l'Echelle, no. 9; J. Frey, place des Victoires, no. 8.

It would seem that even at this late date the singers still had not been
engaged.[6]

The *minutiae* of this news item reveal a bit about the more mundane
preoccupations of the musician. To begin with, the concert-giver seems not to
have considered it inappropriate to handle reservations for the most expensive
seats personally. It is in fact possible that this practice encouraged the purchase
of these tickets, as the act of making arrangements might give the fashionable
an excuse to meet celebrated virtuosi. (To be sure, in most cases servants
probably transacted such business.) The list of ticket outlets is extensive,
making the purchase convenient, although it should not escape notice that the
music shops, Erard's, and Hummel's hotel were all in one quarter of Paris, the area
around the present *Bibliothèque nationale*. The use of three levels of prices suggests
that the single subscription charge of 1825 had been prohibitively inflexible.

---

[6] According to *La Revue Musicale*, March 27, 1830, the singers were a M. Hurteaux and
a Mlle. Minoret, about whom I was able to find no information.

As Hummel's concert approached, newspaper reports became increasingly enthusiastic; Hiller had oiled the publicity machine well. The rarity of any concert publicity in *Le Globe* makes this notice of March 21 stand out from its pages with particular vividness:

> The celebrated Hummel, whose arrival in Paris we announced a few days ago, will give a musical evening in the rue Chantereine on Wednesday the 24th of March. The name of Hummel suffices to attract a crowd; whosoever has tried his hand at the piano owes him respect and recognition. Although his works have only penetrated into France for a few years, one finds them on every piano, and their success is to some extent popular. There are few musical imaginations richer and more abundant than Hummel's. Even while only writing for the piano, he makes one dream of an orchestra, voices, dramatic effects: a simple piece without accompaniment frequently produces impressions of the same type that a symphony of Beethoven makes one feel. This wholly poetic manner of feeling and making his art speak reveals itself above all in improvisation: it is there that Hummel is prodigious and perhaps without rivals. Improvising, for him, is not a work of mechanism and memory; he is not content to take a theme, modulate it and embellish it for a few minutes, then to leave it there to recommence the same operation on a second theme, nay even on a third; no, he seeks a thought, and develops it in all its facets without formulas, without making a patchwork, by an effort totally spontaneous and daring. To be sure these improvisations of the highest purity [*de bon aloi*], if one may so designate them, have a celebrity in Germany that is without equal. It is five years since Hummel made such a short visit to Paris, and all our artists [now] share the admiration of Germany. It is not, I think, adding a feeble allurement to Wednesday's concert, to announce that it will be terminated with one of these beautiful improvisations.

Should we have suspicions about the depth of this enthusiasm, we can always turn for clarification to the response of the vulture-like "arrangement-industry," which was ever ready to capitalize on a famous name through watered-down versions of fine works, for which no fees or royalties were paid to the original composer. This time it cranked out a set of quadrilles on themes from Hummel's ballets, arranged by Alexandre Charles Fessy.

Finally, the long awaited *soirée* materialized, and there was the usual talk of the elegance of Hummel's playing. *La Gazette de France* (March 27) rejoiced, for "never, in truth, has one seen such a brilliant assemblage," and therefore was particularly unhappy that Hummel had had to be content with the relatively small Salle Chantereine. (Presumably Erard's room had been fully booked before his arrival.) The quality of the concert—a matter that reporters usually considered secondary to the social aspects of the occasion—was up to Hummel's usual high standard. Parisians, however, sensitive about the years of rivalry with Britain and its renowned technological wizardry, enjoyed most of all the new piano on which he played, the latest creation of Erard. This instrument, with the improved escapement that had earned for Erard the title "Piano Maker to the King of England," had been built on the personal order of Hummel's patroness, the Duchess of Berry.

Hummel gave one further concert in Paris, on April 3, this time at Erard's. By popular demand, he repeated the Concerto in A flat.[7] The novelty of the program—which also included an oboe solo, vocal music, and an improvisation— was the new *Septetto militaire* (Op. 114). *La Revue Musicale* (April 10) was beside itself with joy after the two concerts, and surpassed its competitors by giving its readers an engraved portrait—"the perfect likeness of which is guaranteed"—of Hummel.

Even such enthusiastic reviews, however, must be interpreted very cautiously. Fétis, the editor of *La Revue Musicale* and apparently a friend of Hummel, revealed a few years later that opinions had been divided: "However much one admired the elegance of his playing, one seemed to detect the approach of old age in a certain timidity of execution that caused him to slow up the tempo noticeably in difficult passages; such, at least, was the judgment borne by pianists." And Fétis' son Edouard, recounting the highlights of the season in *La Revue Musicale* (May 22, 1830), had little to say about Hummel—only that he had had no less pleasure from him than from Moscheles (whom he had liked) and that Hummel had performed some new pieces.

Hummel could not stay around to hear second thoughts. He had already spent more than a month in Paris, and England was his real destination. On April 8 he left for London. According to the ever-present *La Revue Musicale* (April 10; it may have had a direct wire to Hummel), he would spend several months there, go on to Scotland, and return home *via* Paris about the end of September. It was to be a busy time, during which he could gain or lose much. Hummel must therefore have been pleasantly surprised when the best of his Parisian reviews turned up in *The Harmonicon*'s Foreign Musical Report in May—if he himself did not arrange for it!

London Revisited

England's proximity to the Continent would suggest that a foreign musician could easily have built a career there. In fact, Hummel's own experience illustrates how intermittent political turmoil made sustained success there very difficult, but not impossible.

---

[7] Although the general impression in Paris was that the Concerto was new, Hummel had played it at Weimar as early as February 3, 1828, and shortly thereafter in northern Germany and Poland. The Septet, and the Fantasy "Oberons Zauberhorn," published as Opp. 114 and 116, had first been heard at court concerts in Weimar, December 10 and 27, 1829.

He first introduced his own music into England during his prodigy tour, 1790-93. Afterwards, during the ensuing war years, concert life in London was at a low ebb and contact with the Continent severely impaired. Hummel, at that time, was active only in Vienna and Eisenstadt, as a conductor, composer, and teacher. Nevertheless, even though he did not return to the international stage until the end of the war in 1815, England already had a limited knowledge of his music through the pirated editions of his works that were rolling off English presses. Hummel's return to public performing, coinciding, as it happened, with the reopening of communication across the Channel, marked the beginning of his wider reputation in England as a composer. This is clearly visible in English musical journals. In the twelve years from the founding of the first important British music magazine (*The Quarterly Musical Magazine and Review*) in 1818, until Hummel's return there in 1830, his compositions were reviewed by English periodicals no fewer than sixty-six times. Since writers discussed both new music and pirated editions of older works, Hummel's tour was heralded by notice of nearly all of his important compositions. In 1823, *The Quarterly Musical Magazine and Review* could already write that "the works of BEETHOVEN and HUMMEL are now widely diffused in this country, and are perhaps nearly as well known as those of RIES, KALKBRENNER, and MOSCHELES." This comment is particularly significant because the last three were all active in London at the time but Hummel had not been there for decades. Stylistically, Hummel was viewed as the heir of his teacher Mozart, in contrast to Ferdinand Ries, the follower of Beethoven. His music was consistently commended for fine melodic lines, and "scientific"—*i.e.* contrapuntally and harmonically intricate—and tasteful construction. In what the critics of the time called the "piano department," the hallmark was great difficulty. Reviewers liked to group Hummel with Kalkbrenner, Moscheles, Ries, and sometimes with John Field; they dismissed the younger generation of pianists *ca.* 1824 as less "scientific" or "learned" than their elders. In "learnedness" (but, of course, not in personal style), Hummel was placed right by the side of Beethoven, and both were held up as models for the avid student. *The Quarterly Musical Magazine and Review* (VI [1824], 117) exhorted professional and amateur alike to study Hummel's music in order to improve their taste:

> It is considered disgraceful for an amateur of painting to be
> ignorant of the peculiar distinctions between the styles of Raphael,
> Titian, Guido, Claude, &c. Why then, is it not equally desirable for
> a musical virtuoso to be acquainted with the manner of Hummel,
> Von Weber, Mayseder. . . .

The use of Hummel as a model for the elevation of taste is a thread running through English criticism at this time, and nowhere was the mission of improving public sensibilities pursued with greater vigor than in the new journal of 1823, *The Harmonicon.* In this respect it is interesting to see that in June, 1824, the editor, William Ayrton, considered Hummel important enough to make him the subject of one of the monthly biographical "memoirs" with accompanying engraved portrait. Hummel's was the seventeenth; the others had been, in order of appearance, Haydn, Mozart, Cimarosa, J.S. Bach, Purcell, Gluck, Handel, Rossini, Beethoven, Salieri, Cramer, Paisiello, Weber, Ries, Viotti, and Corelli. *The Harmonicon*'s memoir—the first of a living, non-resident, and primarily instrumental composer—summarizes Hummel's standing among English musical journalists:

> The most brilliant aera in the history of German music singularly
> coincides with the golden age of its poetry. At the time when, in
> the *north* of Germany, Klopstock, Wieland, Schiller and Goëthe
> [*sic*], produced those sublime works which surpassed all that the
> German muse ever brought to light, Haydn, Mozart, and Beethoven,
> saved the reputation of the *south*, by producing in the sister art
> immortal compositions in a universal language, that will hand down
> their names to all posterity. Each art has yet, it is true, its
> representatives in Goëthe and Beethoven; but, like setting suns, they
> no longer shine with meridian brilliancy. As both arts were about
> the same time in their zenith, so both have been contemporaneously
> on the decline. The makers of verses and the composers of passages,
> have as much increased, as the inventors of poetical ideas, and of
> melodies, have diminished. But,—not to continue the parallel any
> further,—the few living musicians of Germany who form an exception
> to this assertion, and from whom the preservation of classical taste
> must be expected, belong nearly all to the old school. Spohr, Hummel,
> C.M. von Weber, were not only contemporaries of those great German
> composers, but lived in the same town, and in friendly intercourse
> with them. How beneficially this must have influenced their musical
> education is self-evident. None of them had, however, in this respect,
> greater advantages than Hummel [*i.e.* his studies with Mozart and his
> personal contact with Haydn and Beethoven]. . . .

The writer then gave a most laudatory account of Hummel's life and works. It is noteworthy that he either knew or knew of the full range of Hummel's music: the list of compositions at the conclusion of the Memoir even includes pieces for the stage that are to this day unpublished.[8] Of this long list, he felt that the Septet, Op. 74, the Piano Concerto in A-minor, Op. 85, and the "Grand Duo" for piano four-hands (presumably Op. 92) were Hummel's most significant compositions; oddly enough, the first two were about the only pieces by Hummel

---

[8] The source of the information could have been Continental periodicals, personal experience of the writer, or information provided by any one of the numerous foreign musicians in England, such as Moscheles (whom the author of the Memoir considered to be Hummel's only rival as a pianist). Frimmel says that some *Harmonicon* memoirs were written by a Mr. Schultz (*Beethoven Forschung*, [10 vols.; Vienna: Gerold *et al.*, 1911-1925], X, 50). As this Schultz appears to be the same person for whom Hummel wrote many works on commission after 1819 (see below), any responsibility he might have taken to present a Memoir of Hummel would have served his own interests as well. A connection between Schultz and the Memoir of Hummel could not be proven, however. The Sainsbury dictionary of 1824 also included a substantial article on Hummel.

to remain in the repertoire from his death until the present. Unfortunately, while generally well-informed, this Memoir also contains certain remarks that, although not so ill-intended in context, were to cause trouble later, when other authors used it undiscriminatingly as a source of biographical information:

> As a composer Hummel ranks very high, though it is principally on his Piano-forte works that his reputation rests. He is certainly not over scrupulous in availing himself of the materials of other masters, but like a man of taste, he interweaves them so skillfully with his own, that there is nothing heterogeneous in the composition of the whole. From no other composer has he borrowed so freely as from his own master—Mozart; and it requires no great ingenuity to discover the similarity in their Piano-forte works. Those of Hummel are much more brilliant and difficult, owing to the progress which Piano-forte playing has made within the last ten years. . .

The Memoir's conclusion touched upon a favorite preoccupation of English writers on foreign musicians:

> Having always been very prudent in the management of his affairs, M. Hummel is now in the possession of an independent fortune, such as enables him to keep a carriage, and to live in every other respect in the style of the opulent and the great.

The English amateurs would have had no trouble following the advice to acquaint themselves with Hummel's music, for scores were freely available in England. All compositions published after 1826 (the Mass Op. 111 excepted) appeared in authorized English editions.[9] Since London dealers imported Continental publications, those works published earlier were also easily obtainable. John Ewer and Co., advertising in *The Harmonicon* (January, 1824), even claimed to stock *all* the works of the most esteemed composers, one of whom was Hummel. The dealers were probably selling imported authentic and pirated editions, and certainly the home-grown piracies, through which most of Hummel's earlier works were accessible. A copy of the Piano Sonata Op. 13 in Pleyel's pirated edition and with the stamp "R. Cocks & Co./Importers of/ Foreign Music/29 Princes St. Hanover Sq." is only one of many similar examples now in the British Library. Furthermore, because many music companies had offices in Edinburgh, Dublin, *etc.*, all editions could be had throughout the United Kingdom (and music could, of course, be shipped). The subscribers' list to the English edition of the *Piano Method* shows the wide circulation of works costing as much as three or four pounds,[10] for the following "music warehouses" and "booksellers" (in London unless otherwise indicated) had reserved copies:

---

[9] For a full discussion of English and French editions, see this author's "Authentic English and French Editions of J.N. Hummel," *op. cit.*

[10] I have not found a copy containing the price. The English edition was advertised by Haslinger as being available in Vienna at thirty florins (about three pounds). Farrenc's French edition cost 100 francs, about £3.15.0. Boosey's reissue of the work (1830) was advertised at 3 guineas. (A guinea was one pound and one shilling, £1.05 in modern currency.)

Betts (3 copies)
Bianchi, Ipswich
Blumfield, Hull
Booth, Leeds
Bowcher, Chester
Clementi and Co. (2 copies)
Cocks and Co.
Davies, Southampton
Davis, Portsmouth
Goulding and Co. (2 copies)
Hodges, Bristol
Howell, Bristol
Leader, Bath
Mason, Newcastle-under-Lyme
Muff, Leeds
Paterson, Roy and Co., Edinburgh (2 copies)
Payne and Hopkins [Paine and Hopkins] (8 copies)
Penny and Son, Sherborne
Preston
Richardson, Newcastle
Robertson, Mr. A., Edinburgh (6 copies)
Robinson, Mr. John, York
Rolls, Plymouth
Sabin, Birmingham
Vernon
Weiss, W.G., Liverpool
Welch, T. (Harmonic Institution) [Welsh]
Wooley, Nottingham

In addition to the various pirated editions of Hummel's older works, many compositions and arrangements were being freshly commissioned for England and appeared there in a steady flow throughout the 1820's. In fact, most of his compositions of this period were destined for London, and particularly for a resident German [?], J.R. Schultz, who bought them on speculation and resold them for publication. [11] Hummel's status "in print" was summarized by *The Harmonicon* (March, 1824) in reviewing a Potpourri for piano and harp:[12]

---

[11] For more about these compositions, see the conclusion and Appendix. Regarding Schultz, see Alan Tyson, "J.R. Schultz and his visit to Beethoven," *Musical Times*, May, 1972, pp. 450-451. Dr. Tyson shows that J.R. Schultz was probably Johann Reinhold Schultz, an author and apparently very learned gentleman. According to the documents of the Philharmonic Society, he was in partnership with Thomas Boosey, the publisher. Further on his relations with Hummel, see Sachs, "Authentic English and French Editions of Hummel" and "Hummel and the Pirates." See also above, p. 37 fn. 8, and p. 55.

[12] Probably an unauthorized arrangement of Op. 79; the harp part was arranged by Moscheles from a guitar part.

"As the name of Hummel is becoming very fashionable, we expect to hear that his present work obtains an extensive sale."

Hummel would have doubtless been pleased to know how well his compositions were selling in Britain. It is even more instructive to observe the increasing frequency with which his music was being publicly performed. The most prestigious forum was, of course, the Philharmonic Society.[13] The first piece by Hummel to be heard at the Philharmonic was the popular Septet, Op. 74, the major work on the opening concert of the 1818 season; Charles Neate was the pianist, with Ireland (flute), F. Griesbach (oboe), C. Tully (horn), Spagnoletti (viola), R. Lindley (cello), and D. Dragonetti (bass). The program claims (probably with justification) that it was the first performance of the Septet in England. (Neate himself may have brought the Septet to London, for he was studying in Vienna when Hummel first played it in January, 1815, and could have been present for the premiere.) In the 1820 season, Messrs. J. Beale, Spagnoletti, and R. Lindley played an unspecified Trio for piano, violin, and cello, probably Op. 83, which had been published by Boosey in 1819. By 1821, when Neate played the Piano Fantasy, Op. 18 (first concert), and repeated the Septet (sixth concert, with a different horn player and violist), Hummel was well established on the Philharmonic programs, amidst Haydn and Beethoven symphonies, and Italian vocal music. Success at the Philharmonic cannot be extrapolated to a generalization, however. The London Tavern Amateur Concerts (1819-22) was one series at which no music by Hummel was heard. This seems paradoxical, since the concerts were directed by the same Sir George Smart who virtually controlled the Philharmonic and nearly every other important concert in London. Apparently in the City the prevailing fashions favored Mozart, Rossini, and other Italian vocal composers, past (mostly) and present.[14]

During the rest of the 1820's, Hummel's music was a staple of the Philharmonic Society's repertoire. Yet strangely enough, although the Philharmonic programs included ensemble music of all genres, between the season of 1821 and the time of his tours. Hummel was represented there only by the first Septet and two Piano Concertos:

> 1822. First concert (February 25). Concerto (unspecified in the program), played by Henry Field of Bath (no relative of John Field). First performance in England.[15]

The *Allgemeine musikalische Zeitung*'s correspondent wrote that Field's excellent performance was no mean feat, for playing Hummel on the

---

[13] All programs may be found in Myles Birket Foster, *History of the Philharmonic Society of London: 1813-1912,* (London: Lane, 1912).

[14] Program: Lbm, C.61.h(2), with marginalia in Sir George's hand.

[15] According to Sir George Smart (Lbm, Add. 41,779, f. 11).

stiff-actioned Broadwood was like playing a Mayseder violin Rondo on the double bass.[16]

> 1822. Fifth concert (April 29). Concerto, B-minor, played by Lucy Philpot Anderson.

One of the first female professional pianists, Lucy Anderson was a frequent soloist at the Philharmonic Society. Alas, at this, her Philharmonic debut, "from some of those accountable chances which attend public exhibitions, her merits were not appreciated."[17]

> 1824. Sixth concert (May 10). Concerto (unspecified in the program), Mme. Szymanowska, piano. Another debut.

The *Allgemeine musikalische Zeitung* informs us that she played the A-minor Concerto. Both her performance and the Concerto were sensations, according to *The Harmonicon, The Quarterly Musical Magazine,* and the Leipzig *Allgemeine musikalische Zeitung.*

> 1827. First concert (February 18), and seventh concert (May 21).

M.B. Foster writes of these, "[In the 1827 season] both L. Schlesinger [a student of Ries], and the great Liszt, here described as 'Mr. Liszt,' made their first appearances, playing in both cases, a Concerto of Hummel. How this custom arose is a puzzle, but for some time it seemed as necessary a tradition to begin your career with the Philharmonic Society by playing a Hummel Concerto as it became the fashion and test of a *prima donna* to make her first venture as Marguerite in Gounod's 'Faust'."[18]

The origin of this custom of making debuts with Hummel's Concertos is not puzzling, given his reputation. The fashion was already entrenched on the Continent by 1820. Liszt had played Hummel Concertos in Pressburg and Vienna at the age of eleven, and the Septet, Op. 74, remained in his performing repertoire

---

16 June 19, 1822. Hummel himself remarked that he preferred not playing on the more resistant English action. He did not say, however, that he disapproved of English piano construction. He felt rather that one should remain with that instrument on which one had been trained, in order to reach artistic goals most easily. (Letter to J.B. Streicher, December 15, 1836. Original: Wn, Hs. 126/66-1; printed in Benyovszky, pp. 285-86.) Amusingly enough, a Mayseder violin Rondo was played as a double-bass solo in an 1861 Philharmonic concert! Concerning H. Field, see Leipzig *Allg. mus. Ztg.*, July 26, 1837.

17 *Quarterly Musical Magazine and Review,* IV (1822), pp. 252-53. Mrs. Anderson (1797-1850) was the wife of George Anderson, Master of the Queen's Musick from 1848 to 1870. She was one of the most active pianists of either sex and counted Queen Victoria among her students.

18 Foster, p. 82. *The Harmonicon* (June, 1827) wrote of Liszt's performance, "The only drawback to this piece of music, and to the manner of executing it, was a passage of notes running up and down the scale, which, though much too long in itself, Mr. Lizst [*sic*] prolonged by repetitions that were his own, if we are not much mistaken. This, however, was a trifling fault, and fully redeemed by the indisputable merit of the performance, taken as a whole."

at least into the 1840's, when it was considered a standard "classic." It became a tradition that lasted well into the century; among the later prodigies to observe it was César Franck.

Returning to the Philharmonic, we find the D-minor Septet again, on the third concert of the 1827 season (March 19), played by Mrs. Anderson, and Messrs. Nicholson (flute), Ling (oboe), Platt (horn), Moralt (viola), R. Lindley (cello) and Dragonetti (bass). And the Concerto in B-minor formed the centerpiece of the fifth program of 1829 (April 27), played by Mr. L. Schlesinger. Of this *The Athenaeum* wrote on May 6:

> The whole assimilated remarkably well, considering, the difficulty
> of the composition: a few flat ninths were not *quite* well in tune,
> but if a writer will venture unusual and extraneous modulations
> upon such instruments [the four french horns in the slow
> movement] he must expect a little 'contrary wind' occasionally.

Hummel's music was also heard at "Benefit" concerts, programs similar to those he had given in Paris. Promoted by a single musician for his own profit, they contained a mixture of vocal and instrumental selections performed with the assistance of professionals and amateurs. One of the earliest to include a piece by Hummel was J.B. Cramer's of Friday, July 6, 1823, at Willis's Rooms, where Cramer and Kalkbrenner played a four-hands composition, probably Op. 92. This was good exposure for Hummel's music, for, according to the Leipzig *Allgemeine musikalische Zeitung* (September 3), the concert was jammed, with at least 150 standing. How much of the performance was in accordance with Hummel's intentions is another question, for the Leipzig newspaper complained that Kalkbrenner, who played the top part, added ornaments that were not wholly in keeping with the work's "purely classical spirit."

As on the Continent, the Benefit world was to a great extent the world of the prodigy. In 1824 another one added himself to the list of those known for playing Hummel's music: the eleven-year old George Aspull.[19] This young man was being touted as the English Liszt and was becoming quite a celebrity; he had already been exhibited for the King at Windsor, performing "the more elaborate pieces of Beethoven, Mozart, Hummel, Kalkbrenner, Moscheles, Kreutzer, and Clementi..."[20] In a Benefit on June 15, he played Hummel's Polonaise Op. 55 (as well as a Czerny Concerto and pieces by Mozart).[21] Other Hummel interpreters included youths at the newly-founded Royal Academy of Music.

---

[19] Aspull was born in Manchester, June 1813, and died in Leamington, August 19, 1832. "After a visit to Paris in April 1825 George undertook a number of concert tours throughout Great Britain and Ireland. In spite of his death at the age of nineteen, he was extraordinarily famous. He is credited with having given the first performance in England of Weber's 'Concertstück'." (*Grove's*, 5th ed.) Aspull could have met Hummel in Paris.

[20] *The Harmonicon*, March 1824.

[21] *Wiener Zeitschrift...*, July 3, 1824; *The Harmonicon*, March 1824.

In their concerts were heard his Concertos, the Septet, a Rondo with orchestra—probably Op. 56—and the first English performance of the four-hands Nocturne, Op. 99 (without, however, the two *ad lib*. horns).

In the later 1820's, Hummel's music acquired other distinguished performers. One of these, Ignaz Moscheles, whose programming was always innovative, gave the first English performances of the Concerto Op. 110 at his 1826 Benefit; he probably had obtained it the previous year when he saw the composer, an old friend, in Paris. Lucy Anderson, now finally at the highest ranks of London's performers, was also still a Hummelite. She played Concertos, *La Sentinelle*, Op. 71, and other unidentified compositions by him at Benefits in 1826, 1828, and 1829.

With two first English performances at this time, Hummel finally penetrated the conservative world of provincial festivals. The fifth concert of the Norwich Festival, September 18-21, 1827, featured the Sanctus, Benedictus, and Hosannah of the Mass in E flat, Op. 80, "never performed in this kingdom." The novelty of sacred music by Hummel did not pass unappreciated, as *The Quarterly Musical Magazine and Review* indicated with syntax convoluted even by its own standards:

> The Mass music, especially that of Hummell [*sic*], was
> exceedingly interesting, from the contrast it afforded to those
> pieces with which though we cannot dispense, have yet been
> so often repeated as to leave nothing to the imagination.

Another festival, the Yorkshire Amateur Meeting, July 25, 1826, included what may have been the British premiere of the Overture Op. 101.

From the other domains of British music, the private concert and amateur music-making, few details of any sort survive. Regarding Hummel's works in particular, information is virtually non-existent. I could find only two references to his music. Letters to Dragonetti indicate that he was called upon to assist in readings of the Septet at the home of Thomas Alsager, proprietor of *The Times* and a keen amateur musician;[22] and the Edinburgh publisher George Thomson told Hummel of playing his Piano Trios and Sonatas (for piano and flute, violin, or viola) at his home.[23]

The preceding mass of data suggests that by the time of the 1830 tour, England "knew" Hummel well. A great variety of his music was being performed, introduced by both Continentals and the most noted English musicians

---

[22] Lbm, Add. 17,838, f. 14, letter from Alsager.
[23] See Sachs, "Hummel and George Thomson," *op. cit.*

(of all ages); performances of new pieces came shortly after their publication or even when the music was still in manuscript; for those who wished to study or play his works, imported and local editions—especially cheap piracies—were freely available; musical periodicals often discussed Hummel and his compositions; and English publishers provided him with a stream of commissions. In short, Hummel had every reason to expect a fine reception.

He arrived in England April 9 or 10, and immediately set about arranging his affairs. This was facilitated by the presence of some old friends and acquaintances among the foreigners dominating London's musical life. Moscheles was particularly helpful as a guide through the maze of local customs and musical politics. In the publishing world he had J.R. Schultz, who for a decade, as we have seen, had commissioned many new works (such as the Trio Op. 83), and pianist-composer-publisher J.B. Cramer. Although German by birth, Cramer was fully English, and one of the best-placed men in London's musical power structure. While no correspondence between Hummel and Cramer is extant, the two were certainly acquainted, having met at least once, in Vienna in 1798 (when Hummel is said to have declared that he never heard anyone play Beethoven's music better than Cramer).[24] Their exchange of dedications (Hummel's Trio Op. 83 and Cramer's Piano Sonata Op. 63), about 1819 suggests another meeting. Cramer showed his respect for Hummel in the preface of his *Studies for Piano*, printed in *The Musical Library*, 1835:

> If musicians have a desire to exalt their art, and to procure for
> it the protection and esteem of a learned and enlightened public,
> let them promote, by every means in their power, the cultivation
> of the works of the great masters,—Handel, Haydn, Mozart,
> Beethoven, Weber, Hummel, &c.—composers who have not thought
> it sufficient, merely to captivate the ear, but have endeavoured to
> elevate the mind and satisfy the judgment, by grandeur of sentiment
> and dignity of expression.

In addition to Schultz and Cramer, there were others who could assist Hummel. The English office of the Erard company was one; another was Vincent Novello, a distinguished composer, arranger, publisher, and organist of the Portuguese Embassy. Novello seems not to have met Hummel before the tour, but in the summer of 1829 he had visited Germany and Austria in order to take up a collection for Mozart's impoverished sister, and would certainly have attempted to contact Mozart's most famous and affluent student while in Saxony.[25] Finally, there was the aged Muzio Clementi, with whom Hummel is even said to have studied as a child;[26] they

---

[24] Thea Schlesinger, *Johann Baptist Cramer und seine Klaviersonaten* (diss., Munich 1928), pp. 47-48.

[25] The trip is discussed in a letter from Novello to Dragonetti, June 11, 1829, Lbm, Add. 17,838, ff. 243-44.

[26] Carl Czerny, "Recollections from My Life," trans. Ernest Sanders, *The Musical Quarterly*, XLII (1956), p. 308-9. There is no other evidence that Hummel studied with Clementi; Hummel himself never mentioned it. At least one of Hummel's students in Weimar was English, a Mr. Hodges of Bristol. (Benyovszky, p. 216).

had last seen one another years earlier, when Hummel played in Frankfurt, November 14, 1817.[27]

All of these people were essentially part of the commercial world of music. But in England—unlike France—an entrée into aristocratic circles was also considered useful, for if music was not loved by the upper class, it was at least regarded as fashionable. In this pursuit Hummel had an advantage: the highest levels of society were made more accessible to him because the Engish royalty was of German background, and Hummel was on good terms with the German aristocracy. King George IV had already received (*i.e.* paid for) the dedication of the English edition of the *Piano Method* in 1828;[28] Hummel, as we shall observe, would soon obtain even greater benefits from Adelaide, Duchess of Clarence, born Duchess of Saxe-Meiningen, whose sister married a Weimar Duke.

In theory, this trip had been arranged for the best possible dates. Indeed, there was little leeway, for despite its intensity, London's musical season was actually short. Its duration was limited by the tendency of the political, commercial, and aristocratic leaders—who formed its "exclusive" audience—to desert the capital when Parliament was not sitting. Concerts were therefore traditionally reserved for the spring, and Hummel had arrived at the height of the season. As fate would have it, however, he had picked a poor year. The upper classes were nervous about parliamentary reform and the Catholic and Jewish rights bills, and court gaieties were dampened by the King's protracted illness. Nevertheless, these discouraging signs did not prevent Hummel from arranging his first Benefit—a so-called "Morning Concert" (2 P.M.)—for April 29, at the Concert Room of the King's Theatre (in the Haymarket). The featured attractions were "a new ms. Concerto [presumably Op. 113]—a Grand Characteristic Fantasia, and an Extemporaneous Performance on the Grand Piano-Forte."[29] The usual vocal and instrumental miscellany, with such performers as the great soprano Margarete Stockhausen, were to provide diversion.

As Hummel's concerts near, we find ample material for a view of his publicity techniques. Among the commercially-minded English there was no need to disguise advertising as news, and the first advertisement appeared only a week after Hummel's arrival. The autograph of a letter from Hummel to the Sunday newspaper *John Bull* shows that there was no manager or public-relations officer. Hummel wrote his own copy, carefully stressing that certain words be underlined.[30] He must have had very modern feelings about the value of

---

[27] Leipzig *Allg. mus. Ztg.,* December 17, 1817.

[28] Acceptance of dedications was a duty of the Marquess of Conyngham, Lord Steward of the King's Household. In the case of the *Piano Method*, Christian Kramer (?-?), music director to the King at Windsor, was an intermediary between Hummel and the Royal Household. In a letter dated November 7, 1827, he informed Hummel that the King had accepted the dedication. (Original: MH.)

[29] *John Bull*, April 25, 1830.

[30] Lbm, Add. 33,965, f. 318. Partly printed, but without the instructions, Benyovszky, p. 277.

publicity and appears to have outspent all his colleagues for newspaper insertions. Aiming for broad coverage, he bought space in the dailies *The Times* and *The Morning Chronicle*, the Sunday edition of *John Bull*, and even in *The Court Journal*, a magazine of fashion, literature, arts, and events in the aristocratic world[31] that few other musicians considered a worthwhile medium. Hummel's advertisements appeared about ten days before the concert and once more on the day itself. As in Paris, the first notice usually gave only the date and a hint of the program.

In addition to newspaper advertising, there was another form of publicity, which Hummel may also have used. Fétis described it in 1829, in a letter translated in *The Harmonicon* (November):

> ...enormous bills, and smaller ones distributed in the [concert] rooms, and even in the streets,—are constantly resorted to. Here it is not permitted to post bills on the walls, but they are found at the music venders, the grocers, and even on the back of a sheep in a butcher's shop.

Publicity was, of course, only the beginning of Hummel's costs, and considering the many expenses that Hummel must have incurred, it is unfortunate that so few details have survived. Some estimates may be made, however, on the basis of documents of the Philharmonic Society.[32] To begin with, as the Philharmonic Society paid 240 guineas for the use of the Concert Room for eight concerts and eight rehearsals, we may estimate that Hummel paid about thirty guineas to rent the hall for his Benefit. An approximation of his musical expenses is also possible. Presuming that he used an orchestra of no more than fifty, and judging from London's standard fees, assisting instrumentalists would have cost him about £100.[33] The Philharmonic accounts and the papers of Sir George Smart indicate that vocal soloists were normally paid ten to fifteen guineas. Total expenses for a full-scale Benefit, including advertising, were therefore probably on the order of £200. Since the capacity of the Concert Room was about 800,[34] with tickets sold at one-half a guinea (10s. 6d.), Hummel's profit

---

[31] According to the Leipzig *Allg. mus. Ztg.* (April 16, 1823), *John Bull* and *The Morning Chronicle* were the two general newspapers read by all London's music lovers. Although tastes undoubtedly fluctuated over the years following that item, these two remained the newspapers most generally cited in discussions of music in London. (*John Bull* also had a Monday edition, mostly financial news.) It was to be some time before *The Times* included much musical news.

[32] Papers of the Society, Lbm, Loan 48, *passim.*

[33] Largely from Smart papers, Lbm, Add. 41,777 *passim.*

[34] I have been unable to find the exact capacity of the Concert Room of the King's Theatre. The figure 800 is a rough estimate based on architectural drawings. The plans show that the room—which was on the same level as the first tier of boxes in the main auditorium (Opera House)—had a level floor and one small, rectangular balcony with about five rows of seats. The arrangement was about the same as that in Carnegie Recital Hall, New York, and the Wigmore Hall, London. The floor area was, however, considerably larger than these two. Plans are printed as an appendix to Charles Dibdin, *History and Illustrations of the London Theatres,* (London: "Illustrations of London Buildings," 1826).

could have been as much as £200. As in Paris, however, not everyone paid for tickets. Nevertheless, Hummel's friends did their best to help. Moscheles wrote in his diary, "Hummel is here, he wants to give a concert, and I am so happy to be able to sell many tickets for him among my [female!] students.[35]

Hummel's concert took place as scheduled, and left in its wake abundant commentary. The sheer number of reviews of the concert is most impressive: they appeared in *The Times, The Athenaeum,* and *The Spectator*—none of which ordinarily gave extensive coverage to musical events other than opera—and *The Harmonicon.* An article in *The Athenaeum* was indeed unusual, for Hummel was the first instrumentalist other than Paganini to receive significant mention in that primarily literary and political weekly. The critics all paid attention to little other than the three performances by Hummel himself—the Concerto in A-flat, the Fantasy with orchestra (*Oberons Zauberhorn*), and an improvisation employing themes from *Don Giovanni. The Spectator* went so far as to say,

> The other parts of the concert were merely intended to fill up
> the intervals between the different pieces we have mentioned;
> but surely there was no need to insert such mere trash as the
> duet of AUBER-HUMMEL needed no foil of this kind.

They were uniformly enthusiastic about Hummel's playing, particularly his improvising. In their general assessment of Hummel's compositions, they spoke of the now-familiar qualities: good taste, "science," elegance, and so forth. *The Spectator*'s reviewer was unusual in pleading to hear more of Hummel's vocal music. *The Times* and *The Spectator* were not quite correct, however, when they said that the Concerto had been expressly composed for the occasion, since for Hummel the entire concert was merely a repetition of the one given in Paris, March 24.

Having duly absorbed these kind words, we now must unfortunately recall the untrustworthy nature of early nineteenth-century reviews. A bit of reading between the lines causes one to doubt that the evening stimulated unanimous enthusiasm and approval. Take the matter of attendance. According to *The Athenaeum* (May 1) the concert was "well and elegantly attended, although not quite so full as we expected."[36] *The Spectator* (May 1) was more detailed:

> The concert on Thursday had excited an unusual sensation in
> the musical world. Not indeed among the titled and whiskered
> dilettanti; for them the school of HAYDN and MOZART has few
> charms. A school of which intellect and thought are the
> foundation—which appeals to the heart and disdains all false and
> meretricious decoration—is above their reach. But such an

---

[35] Charlotte Moscheles (ed.), *Aus Moscheles' Leben*, (2 vols.; Leipzig: Duncker und Humblot, 1872-1873), I, 222.

[36] The newspapers indicate that weather was good for Hummel's concert: high, 69°; clear; wind, SE.

assemblage of real musical talent we have rarely seen congregated
on any former occasion; there was scarcely a professor of eminence
absent: and we are confident that every anticipation was gratified.

To use that era's euphemism, the audience was probably not large but
"select"! It is also clear that in their reviews of Hummel's concerts, London's
newspapers aligned themselves with the faction defending the traditions of
"science," "elegance," and "beauty" against supporters of modern virtuosity.
Since their praise took the form of a defense of Hummel against the Continental
invasion represented by Henri Herz, Rossini, the newer Italian opera composers,
and singers in general—even Chopin at first was attacked as an exponent of
meaningless virtuosity—we can infer that the London audience was divided in its
reaction to Hummel. *The Athenaeum*'s comments (May 1) illuminate reservations
of at least one faction of the audience:

HUMMEL'S CONCERT

We had on Thursday the gratification of hearing, for the first
time, the pianist who has long been spoken of as the greatest of
his time. Hummel's style of playing appears to us decidedly that
of Cramer; there is the same perfection of finish—the same classical
attention to time—the same delicacy and elegance of ornament,
always appropriate—never superfluous. With all these attributes of
excellence, there is, in addition, so much more force and energy,
that on the whole we certainly regard it as the most sensible and
best, consequently the most effective, pianoforte performance we
have ever heard. There are professors, both here and in Paris, who
perform, or at least attempt, much greater difficulties than did
Hummel on Thursday; and there might be some of his hearers
(admirers of the very new and extravagant school) who would say
there was not a sufficient display of mechanical power, or in other
words, not enough *tours de force*. The impression which his
performance left on us, however, is, that he could execute as much
as anybody, but that his good sense has taught him that the
majority of his audience will be better satisfied with the perfect
accomplishment of as much as can possibly be desired or
understood, than if their ears and understandings are taxed beyond
their comprehension, and their fears of a failure excited by
exertions that are evidently over-strained and laborious, and
consequently painful instead of pleasurable in their effect.
To this we may add, that, with as much execution as is desirable,
or perhaps endurable, there is in Hummel's playing a delightful
ease, an unaffected precision, which convey to his auditors a
certainty of his complete success, and a conviction that the artist
is quite equal to much more than he chooses to attempt. Speaking
of Mr. Hummel as a composer, we may say that his new Concerto
in A flat, is scientific enough to gratify the most fastidious
musician, and sufficiently sweet and graceful (especially the first
and last movements), to charm those amateurs who may not have

had leisure or inclination to adverture beyond a love of melody. The second piece, an introduction and fantasia on a Turkish or Indian air, which we remember in Weber's "Oberon," did not by any means delight us; and we suspect, from the difference between that and Hummel's compositions in general, that it was written for the express purpose of exhibiting some of those tricks and difficulties, which his good taste deemed it unnecessary to display in the Concerto.

We hope this error in judgment will prove a solitary instance of departure from that purity and unequalled perfection of style which has created, and will, without adventitious aid, maintain the well-merited eminence of his musical reputation. The concluding performance was extemporaneous, introducing, "Là ci darem la mano," and "Fin ch'han dal vino," from Mozart's "Don Giovanni." We will not attempt to express our perfect satisfaction at this spontaneous and extraordinary combination of sound and sense, of which every evanescent note left a regret on our minds, that we had not the means of perpetuating its delightful impression. We conclude by stating our conviction that those who have heard Hummel, will not be content without hearing him again, and that for those who have not, there is so much real pleasure in reserve, that we sincerely recommend them to take the earliest opportunity of obtaining it. The Concert, which was at the Opera Rooms, was well and elegantly attended, although not quite so fully as we expected.

Considering that Hummel would have known of English attachment to *Oberon* and that he composed the Fantasy for this tour, we may assume that his so-called lapse of taste was definitely a deliberate catering to the well-known English passion for virtuosity. *The Times* (April 30) did not find it disturbing. To its critic, all Hummel's performances and compositions "fully vindicated the fame which had long preceded his arrival in this country."

We can see, then, that feelings about Hummel were quite mixed. Nevertheless, the absence of the "titled and whiskered" dilettanti must not have seemed a serious omen, for Hummel soon announced a second appearance:

MR. HUMMEL has the honour to inform the Nobility, Gentry, & Public in general, that his Second and LAST CONCERT will take place on TUESDAY MORNING the 11th May at the Concert Hall, King's Theatre. Full particulars will be duly announced.

The full particulars appeared the following week. Again stressing the phrase "LAST CONCERT," the second advertisement continued,

Vocal performers—Madame Malibran-Garcia, Madame Stockhausen, Signor Donzelli, and Mr. Phillips.—Principal Instrumental Performers—Messrs. Mori, Lindley, Dragonetti, Nicholson, William, and Harper. Madame Malibran will sing a new MS. Tyrolean Air with variations, expressly composed for her by Mr. Hummel, who will introduce, in the course of the Concert, a new MS. Septetto Militaire, composed for this occasion; a Grand Sonata by Mozart for two Piano-fortes,

with Mr. Moscheles, who has kindly promised his assistance; and an
Extemporaneous Performance on the Piano-forte, on which occasion
Mr. Hummel requests any of the Company to give him a written
theme to perform on. Tickets, 10s. 6d. each. . . .[37]

The Tyrolean Air and Variations (published as Op. 118) may in fact have been
composed especially for this concert! At this event, according to *The Spectator,*
two (unidentified) vocal duets by Hummel were also sung (and considered
unworthy of Hummel). From *John Bull* we learn that the A-flat Concerto was
added as an encore by popular demand—no mean reward for a receptive audience.
The players in the Septet were drawn from the Philharmonic.

What was the result of Hummel's request for a subject upon which to
extemporise? *The Athenaeum*'s account (May 15) gives us a rare, relatively
detailed description of a Hummel improvisation:

> In compliance with the request in the bill, which was read by
> Sir George Smart, and seconded, in very tolerable English, by
> Mr. Hummel, two themes were offered by some of the audience;—
> the first, a *ranz des Vaches*, or Swiss air, (which, by the way, we
> are rather tired of);—the second, a few bars of something, we
> could not exactly understand of what description, but certainly
> not melody—an extract, we suspect, from some very inferior
> German production. Mr. Hummel appeared somewhat discouraged
> by the unprofitableness of the materials presented to him, but,
> of course, did not reject them. We wish he had done so. He
> commenced with an introductory adagio, followed by some light
> and playful variations on the Swiss air, he modulated through a
> variety of keys into an elaborate fugue, in the progress of which
> he displayed all the enthusiasm of powerful genius, with the
> consummate art and refinement of the most profound musical
> science. Having submitted to the temporary restraint of the
> second theme, which he dismissed as soon as possible, he gave
> the reins to his imagination, and revelled in the mazes of melody
> and harmony, to the exquisite delight of his audience, and, we
> should suppose, to his entire satisfaction. During this most happy
> inspiration of talent and genius, he occasionally introduced a few
> bars of an old English song, "the flaxen-headed cow-boy," which
> he played and sported with in a manner at once so masterly and
> fascinating, that it might have been listened to for hours without
> a feeling of satiety.[38]

---

[37] *John Bull*, May 9, 1830. The "principal instrumental performers," all members of
the Philharmonic, were heard in the Septet.

[38] Swiss "folk" music had enjoyed a vogue throughout the second half of the 1820's as
a result of the tours of the Rainer family, "Tyrolese minstrels." Every journal in England
was sick of the *genre. The Harmonicon* (January, 1831) described England's plight rather
concisely: "The success of the Rainer family . . . was soon bruited in every part of Europe,
and whoever fancied they had the slightest chance of success, made efforts to visit England,
the paradise of money-hunting foreigners."

(*The Harmonicon* [June], was equally enthusiastic about the improvisation. They identified the English song as William Shield's "The Plough Boy," which had been the theme of Hummel's variations Op. I, no. 1, four decades earlier. [39] The "New Variations" on "The Plough Boy" [Op. 120, no. 1], which appeared shortly afterwards, may well be related to this improvisation—or *vice-versa*.)

All sources agree that the attendance was better at this concert. *The Athenaeum* wrote (May 15):

> A more numerous assemblage of beauty and elegance never honoured the performance of any professor, than that which graced the Opera-room, on Tuesday morning. It was quite full, with a majority, we should suppose, of at least, two to one of ladies.

Hummel had succeeded, in terms of both attendance and critical reaction, which was unanimously in his favor. While we shall temporarily reserve judgment as to whether this unanimity should be attributed to the acclaim of "progressives" or "conservatives," *The Spectator*'s review reveals Hummel's potential vulnerability to changes in fashion:

> There was little variety in his second performance, as compared with the first; and indeed, if there had been, it must have been variety without improvement. Hummel is not a man to produce new sleight-of-hand tricks, or to excite gaping wonder by mere feats of manual dexterity. His playing is precisely what we expected to find it, the result of a genius alive to all the powers of his art, trained in the best of all possible schools—the school in which mind and thought are brought to bear upon every passage, and in which the heart is appealed to through the medium of the senses.

The economics and format of Hummel's two Benefit concerts were typical of a visiting artist's major performances. Obviously such concerts would hardly enrich most musicians, and could easily impoverish them. Part of their purpose, like that of a modern debut recital, was to generate other engagements for which the artist would be paid, and Hummel could expect many such opportunities. In this compressed concert season, there were—according to Fétis' account of

---

[39] *The Harmonicon* (April, 1829) supplied the following comment on the tune, which was from Shield's opera *The Farmer* (1787): "The popular air of Shield, *The Ploughboy*, was converted into an excellent rondo by Dussek, and formed part of one of his early and most admired concertos [Op. 15]. At the public concerts and oratorios he performed it incessantly, and those who could master it   for it was then considered fit only for first-rate players - were expected to produce it in all private parties. Thus it was heard *usque ad nauseam*; consequently soon became vulgar, and then was laid on the shelf." The reviewer was glad to see the tune revived in a recent four-hands arrangement of Dussek's Rondo.

London's musical life [40]—three or four concerts a day, and, as a result, stiff competition for audiences. Since Benefits were organized on short notice, foreign artists with sufficiently impressive reputations were frequently hired to attract crowds, at fees of between fifteen and twenty-five guineas. Certainly not all of these concerts were equally important, and few were reviewed. Perhaps one point of reference is the number considered socially important enough to warrant notice by *The Harmonicon*—about ten to fifteen annually—and the dozen or so directed by the most fashionable conductor, Sir George Smart; [41] these were largely the same events. In view of the unreliability of other evidence, let us assume that there were ten or fifteen truly important Benefits, upon which a great deal of money was lavished. Hummel's appearance in eight of them (other than his own) in the 1830 season therefore substantially attests to his success. In all cases his presence was advertised as a leading attraction. These performances were as follows: [42]

May 5. LUCY ANDERSON.

She and Hummel performed his Grand Duet Op. 92. According to *The Court Journal* (May 8), "As this was Hummel's second appearance in this country, the performance excited much curiosity; but it did not in any high degree gratify that curiosity, as the leading portion of the performance was very properly assigned to the lady, who acquitted herself in a most efficient manner."

May 14. THOMAS GREATOREX.

Greatorex (1758-1831), a composer also skilled in mathematics, astronomy and natural history, had been organist of Westminister Abbey since 1819. In this concert Hummel improvised in the "first act"; *The Harmonicon* (July, 1830) identifies the subject as Handel's "Harmonious Blacksmith."

May 19. EDWARD ELIASON.

The gentleman was a violinist in the Philharmonic Society, according to its account books; he may have been German-born. [43] Eliason was active in orchestral and chamber concerts for the subsequent several decades. The concert was under the patronage of H.R.H. Princess Augusta. Hummel played the Grand Duet again, with Mrs. Anderson.

---

[40] *The Harmonicon*, November 1829 (quoted above, p. 46).
[41] See his accounts, Lbm, Add. 41,772, f. 69.
[42] For additional information regarding reviews, *etc.*, see J. Sachs. *Hummel in England and France, op. cit.*, pp. 60-61. The biographical sketches are based largely on information from *Grove's* especially the first and third editions, and the Philharmonic Society papers, Lbm, Loan 48, *passim.*
[43] *The Harmonicon*, July 1830.

May 21. THOMAS VAUGHAN.

This noted tenor (1782-1843) had sung in the Philharmonic Society's first performance of Beethoven's Ninth Symphony, March 21, 1825. According to the advertisement, Hummel was to play a Piano Concerto; *The Harmonicon* (July) says he played a "grand Rondo" (presumably with orchestra) and conducted his Gradual.

May 24. ROBERT LINDLEY.

Lindley (1776-1855) seems to have been the busiest cellist in London: principal cellist in the opera and all of London's leading concerts as well as a professor at the Royal Academy of Music from its founding in the winter of 1822-23. With the Philharmonic violinist Nicolas Mori and Lindley, Hummel played one of his Trios, probably Op. 83. Mme. Malibran sang Hummel's Tyrolean variations.

June 1. IGNAZ MOSCHELES.

This was probably the most widely advertised concert of the season. The advertisement in *John Bull* said that Hummel and Moscheles would play a duet by Mozart, Mme. Malibran would sing Hummel's Tyrolean variations, and Moscheles would improvise on any written theme submitted. The inspiration for the last is obvious. *The Harmonicon* (July) wrote, "This concert was so excessively crowded that a considerable time elapsed before we could gain admittance to any part of the room. . . ."

June 28. LOUISA DULCKEN.

Mme. Dulcken (1811-1850), a noted pianist, was the younger sister of the German violinist Ferdinand David, and lived in London as a highly successful performer after her marriage in 1828. An advertisement in *John Bull* (June 18) says, "Mr. Hummel has kindly consented to play a Grand Duet for two pianofortes (probably the Mozart duo again) with Mme. Dulcken."[44] No additional information about this event has come to light.

July 5. CHARLES AUGUSTE de BÉRIOT.

The Belgian violinist (1802-1870), a former student of Baillot, was well known to the English for his courtship of Mme. Malibran. *The Times'* advertisement began, "Mr. Hummel (his last appearance in this country) will give an EXTEMPORANEOUS PERFORMANCE at Mr. de BÉRIOT'S MORNING CONCERT on Monday, the 5th of July. . . ."

---

[44] Louise David had played Hummel's A-minor Concerto at the age of twelve in Cassel. (Leipzig *Allg. mus. Ztg*., July 22, 1824.)

One further performance, which was projected but did not take place, is described by Moscheles in his diary. It seems that Cramer invited Hummel to join in his Benefit, but because the newspapers liked to compare Hummel and Cramer to the detriment of the former, Hummel declined to participate, thus snubbing England's favorite and possibly insulting the musical world.

These guest appearances served to advance interests far wider than Hummel's own. Publishers, always alert to free fringe benefits, capitalized on the attendant publicity with stirring title-page proclamations like the one on Cocks' edition of the Op. 92 four-hands Sonata: "As performed by Hummel and Mrs. Anderson, Hummel and Field, Hummel and C.O. Hodges." Once again, however, the edition was a piracy and yielded no profit for Hummel.

Certainly the guest performances at Benefits were lucrative. None of them was so prestige-laden, however, as an appearance with the Philharmonic Society. Contact between this august body and Hummel began, we recall, in 1821. The Minutes Book of the Philharmonic's Directors meetings tells the story of that and subsequent events.[45] The first reference is in the minutes of the Directors' meeting November 2, 1821:

> Resolved, that Mr. [Cipriani] Potter be requested to apply (thro'
> the means of his friend Mr. Schultz) to Mr. Hummel enquiring on
> what terms he would accept an Engagement at the ensuing Concert.

For unknown reasons, this assignment could not be completed. Therefore at their next meeting (November 10) the Directors passed a resolution

> That the Secretary write to Mr. Christian Kramer[46] at the Pavilion
> Brighton, requesting him to enquire of Mr. Hummel his terms for
> writing an Overture, and Performing at any 2 or 3 of the ensuing
> Concerts provided they shall not be on successive nights and
> requiring him to abide by the same conditions as those in the
> agreement of Mr. Kiesewetter relative to his playing at any other
> concerts &c.

Much better luck this time. On the 27th Potter read to the Directors a translation of Kramer's letter to Hummel:

> Most esteemed, celebrated &c. Sir,
>
> When I was lately in Hanover, in the suit of His Majesty, our most
> gracious Sovereign, I met quite unexpectedly my friend Papendick,
> whom I knew enjoyed a free correspondence with you, and I begged
> him to write to you, to learn, if the Directors of the Philharmonic
> Concerts might flatter themselves this Season with your universally
> acknowledged rare talent. When Mr. Papendick told me that your
> answer might not be unfavorable, therefore immediately on my

---

45 Lbm, Loan 48.2 (2). Unpaginated.
46 Regarding Kramer, see above, p. 45 fn. 28.

return here I consulted with the other Directors, & have just
received the most agreeable commission to write to you, though
I have not the honor of enjoying your most valuable acquaintance.
Setting aside all useless ceremony, I shall come directly to the point.

There are 8 Concerts, they commence about the middle of
February & take place every 14 days, excepting Passion Week & the
Easter Week, terminating at the beginning of July. What we wish you
to perform is as follows: 1st the Society is very anxious to possess
an Overture of your Composition, it is understood of course, for a
full orchestra.

2d We are desirous that you should give our *Souls* and *ears* a
feast 3 times in the course of the 8 Concerts by your enchanting
playing. 3d Perhaps one evening when your Overture is performed
it would be requested of you to preside at the Piano.

He then went on to discuss the conditions under which the violinist Christoph
Gottfried Kiesewetter had appeared:

The conditions are, that you must perform at the Philharmonic
Concerts at least once before you can give your benefit Concert,
this is certainly to your advantage. It is also the wish of the
Society that you should not perform at other public Concerts,
without the consent of the same (Society). This is only a prudent
precaution; as you are sufficiently acquainted with London from
former times, to know in the profession (Chicanerie) quibbling
oppositions often exist—. Should concerts be established against
ours, it would be extreme folly in you, when *we invite* you, to
make use of your talent against us; in all the other Musical
Resources of this gigantic city, you are at full liberty, & you may
rely upon it that there will not be the least impediment thrown
in your way. Now I have only to beg of an early & favourable
answer, in which you will have the goodness to name the terms
you expect from the above conditions.

The letter continued with many items irrelevant to this history, but in a post-
script Kramer explained that "Mr. Schultz from Germany" (whom Kramer
identified as Boosey's partner) had originally been asked to write, but apparently
had been too busy, and the Directors, not wanting to lose time, had called on
Kramer. Having engaged the great violinists Spohr and Kiesewetter, they were
now extremely anxious to hire a pianist of equal rank.

They did not get one. The idea might have appealed to Hummel, but the
Directors were much too late. On January 9, William Horsley read to the
Directors a letter from Kramer, stating that "Hummel cannot accept an
engagement, being on his way to Russia." The matter was over, and the Minutes
indicate no subsequent contact with Hummel (although in 1827 the Society's
library ordered a copy of his opera *Mathilde von Guise*). Then, on November 2,
1829, Hummel was recommended for honorary membership (at the same meeting
at which Auber, Lesueur, Meyerbeer, and Onslow were voted the same honor); on
January 16, 1830, he was elected.

The affair with the Philharmonic recommenced in the initial newspaper advertisement (*John Bull*, April 18) for Hummel's debut Benefit:

> MR. HUMMEL, Maitre de Chapelle de la Cour de Saxe Weimar, has the honour to announce to the Nobility, Gentry, and the Public, that his MORNING CONCERT will take place in the GREAT CONCERT ROOM, KING'S THEATRE, on THURSDAY, April 29th, 1830. In the course of the Concert Mr. Hummel will introduce a NEW MS. CONCERTO–a Grand Characteristic Fantasia, and an Extemporaneous Performance on the Grand Piano-Forte. Full particulars will be duly announced...

To our innocent eyes this seems perfectly harmless. Unfortunately, Hummel had unknowingly omitted one crucial item. Moscheles tells us in his diary that he would have advised inserting a phrase to dispel the otherwise automatic assumption that Hummel would also appear at the Philharmonic. In this way Hummel could have avoided giving Philharmonic subscribers the impression that they could forego the Benefit, and he could have held out for a lucrative Philharmonic engagement. Moscheles must have transmitted his suggestion, for the next advertisement (*The Times*, April 28) ended, "To prevent the subscribers of the Philharmonic Concert being disappointed in their expectation of hearing Mr. Hummel, during his short stay in London, Mr. Hummel thinks it his duty to inform them, that he will not play at the above concerts unless a suitable engagement is offered to him by the Directors of that Society."

If the presumptuous tone of the announcement suggests that Hummel should not have written his own advertisements, it nevertheless accurately reflects the confusion surrounding Hummel's relations with the Society at this stage. *The Monthly Musical and Literary Magazine* had told London on April 1 (nearly three weeks before the first of Hummel's advertisements) that Hummel would play with the Philharmonic; *The Athenaeum*, ten days later, claimed that he would perform twice, after Easter. But just one week after that (April 17), *The Athenaeum* had to correct itself:

> Hummel, the celebrated pianist, whose coming we anticipated last week, has since arrived in London; but he will not, as we then stated, play at the Philharmonic Concerts, nor anywhere in public, until after his own Concert, which has already been announced.

Moscheles may have been responsible for setting the story straight. Indeed, the Philharmonic's archives, as we know, do not indicate any contact between Hummel and the Society since the inquiry of 1821. The Directors may have been reacting to these conflicting announcements when, meeting on April 18, they "Resolved that Hummel be offered fifteen guineas to play on the 6th night."[47] The courtship then began in earnest. The next evening, at the fourth

---

[47] Minutes Book, *op. cit.* Present at the meeting: Sir George Smart, Messrs. Henry Bishop, Charles Neate, William Dance, Charles Weichsell.

Philharmonic Concert, while Hummel sat in the Directors' Box to hear Mme. Stockhausen sing the *scena* "Deh, Calma" from his opera *Mathilde von Guise*, a prospective engagement may well have been among the idle chit-chat. He soon received an official letter requesting his services, and while still deciding what to do about the offer, was informed of his election as an honorary member of the Philharmonic Society.[48] This, his latest title, did not influence his decision, however, as the minutes of the Directors' Meeting, May 12, show:

> Letter read from Mr. Hummel thanking the Society for his election as an honorary member.
> Letter read from Mr. Hummel stating he cannot accept the terms offered him.
> Resolved that he be written to enquiring his terms for playing at the next Concert.
> Resolved that should they exceed 25 guineas they not be complied with.[49]

Hummel's reply was given at the next meeting:

> Letter read from Mr. Hummel stating his terms for playing at the Concerts to be 50 guineas. Which the Secretary reported his having immediately replied to declining to engage him.[50]

Word of the refusal spread quickly. *The Athenaeum*, reviewing the sixth Philharmonic Concert in their issue of May 22, wrote,

> Report says that we are to have de Bériot at the ensuing Concert, and that Hummel has been offered twenty-five guineas for one performance, but refuses to play for less than fifty.

The accuracy of the report is stunning considering that Directors' meetings were private. In view of the cronyism in London's musical journalism, we may surmise that the Directors themselves leaked the news in order to preserve their reputations. They knew that the failure of the negotiations would provoke a sharp reaction, for the English were convinced that foreigners provided music only in exchange for picking local pockets clean. The resulting gossip can be inferred from a letter to the editor of *The Harmonicon* (June):

---

[48] Although the election date is clearly established by Hummel's reply (see below), Sir George Smart's papers include a list of honorary members compiled in 1860, on which he has written, "1833 was the *first* year they were elected." (Lbm, Add. 41,779 f. 33). This was repeated by Foster, p. 119. The conflict of dates is made more puzzling by the fact that Continental periodicals announced the election only in 1834, along with that of Mendelssohn, Meyerbeer, Onslow, Lesueur, and Auber. (*Neue Zeitschrift für Musik*, May 22, 1834; *La Gazette Musicale*, May 5, 1834.)

[49] Minutes book, *op. cit.* Present: Dance (chair), Weichsell, Neate, Smart.

[50] *Ibid.*; Bishop was present as well as those at the previous meeting.

May 20th, 1830.

Sir,

The question between the directors of the Philharmonic Society and M. Hummel has created so much conversation in the musical world, has been so openly and freely discussed, that it will not be quite useless or uninteresting to state it impartially in your pages, should you deem the communication worthy of insertion.

When this celebrated professor arrived here, it was naturally enough expected that his services would as early as possible be obtained for one Philharmonic concert at least. He was applied to for this purpose, but certainly not in a manner likely to impress an eminent foreigner with a notion that our professional men are influenced by the rules of very high breeding in their first intercourse with strangers. The application was in the form of a letter from the secretary of the society, instead of having been made in person by one of the directors.

This communication was not expressed in uncivil terms, undoubtedly, though far from courteous in its style. It rather called upon than invited M. Hummel to perform, and in blunt language named fifteen guineas as the remuneration he was to expect. A subsequent note raised this noble sum to the still more magnificent one of twenty. M. Hummel answered neither, and herein was not well advised. It must be an extraordinary letter that is not entitled to a reply; besides which, he lost an opportunity of making the directors sensible that the mode in which they had applied to him was not particularly remarkable for its politeness, or the terms proposed very much distinguished by liberality.

It is said that the sum thus fixed was governed by what other great performers have received for their services; but surely there is a wide difference between resident professors, and visitors who undertake a long and expensive journey—between members of a society who directly or indirectly derive some advantages from it, and strangers who cannot be supposed to take any interest in its concerns. The urbanity of a civilized people ought to have pointed out the distinction; and at all events M. Hummel's terms should first have been ascertained; had they been thought unreasonable, or such as the directors could not feel themselves justified in acceding to, the treaty might silently have been brought to a close, and the character of the society for good manners and generosity remained unblemished.

I am, Sir, &c.
An Associate

While such letters rarely provide impartial expositions of facts, "Associate" was generally well informed. Indeed, the offer actually *had* been determined by the prevailing scale of fees. Philharmonic account-books show that the maximum paid to an instrumentalist that season was fifteen guineas (to J.B. Cramer for performing a Mozart Concerto). Mme. Dulcken, Mrs. Anderson, and de Bériot each received ten guineas, and some—Mrs. Anderson, for one—even played gratuitously from time to time. Among the singers, Mme. Malibran was the best paid: twenty-five guineas for each of three performances, and Mme. Stockhausen received ten guineas for each of two. Although Hummel was right to consider the proffered fee miniscule, the Director's offer had actually been the highest to any soloist since 1823 (before which data are incomplete). Only Mme. Pasta had been paid as much, for performances in 1824 and 1826. By local standards, therefore, Hummel had small grounds for complaint.[51] His grander expectations probably stemmed from Continental rumors about London's gold-plated concert stages.[52]

Our saga reached a simple conclusion: no engagement. But the issue of fees was even more tangled than it appeared on the surface. In 1827, a General Meeting of the Philharmonic Society had accepted a new regulation providing that

> Within three months after the death of any member, there shall be transferred to his legal representatives so much of the Society's stock in the public funds then standing in the names of the trustees as shall be equal to one share, the whole being divided into as many shares as there shall have been members living on the day before such death shall happen.[53]

The result would have been the gradual distribution of the Society's funds among the heirs of the oldest members. The justification for the ruling was intriguingly straightforward:

> As it has been through [the older members'] care and attention the funds of the society have been accumulated, they see no reason why those who come after should profit by the labours of those who have gone before.[54]

This policy unfortunately blatantly contravened the unselfish principles upon which the Society had been founded. Even worse, it was a larger problem than that of principle: those whose heirs would share the leftover funds could swell the annual surplus by reducing such expenditures as fees for soloists and for commissions of new works. Not unexpectedly, by 1829 newspapers were complaining that the Philharmonic's programs were becoming tedious and dull as a result of the financial problems caused by the 1827 ruling.

---

[51] Account book, Lbm, Loan 48.9(1). Wages of orchestral players in 1830, for purposes of comparison: (for ten rehearsals and eight concerts) principal flute, oboe, bassoon, horn, £35; second flute, oboe, bassoon, horn, members of first violin section, £20.6.9; "leader" (*i.e.* principal of first violins), £52; principal bass, Domenico Dragonetti, for only seven concerts and five rehearsals, £56.14.0.

[52] *E.g.* Moscheles wrote to Ignaz Edler von Mosel, a Viennese and also a friend of Hummel, on October 31, 1821, "I am completely satisfied with the fruits of my sojourn in London; however, in order to reach the goal of my trip, it is necessary to make a *Da Capo* in order to assemble the pounds-sterling *per augmentationem.* (Wn, Hs. VII. 144-1.)

[53] Quoted in Robert Elkin, *Royal Philharmonic: The Annals of the Royal Philharmonic Society*, (London: Rider, 1947), p. 12.

[54] From a protest, quoted *ibid.*, p. 13.

The affair with Hummel helped bring the issue to a head. In August, 1830, *The Harmonicon* printed a letter with a familiar signature:

> It having transpired that notice has been given at the Philharmonic
> Society of an intended motion to rescind what I have always called, and
> still continue to denominate, the *spoliation law*, or that law by which
> the funds are to be divided among a few of its aged members,—for such
> would be its effect,—I earnestly implore the independent part of the
> society to assist the good cause, by supporting the effort, to be made
> at the next meeting, to redeem the character of the society, which has
> suffered much in public opinion ever since it came to so unjust and
> unwise a resolution, and now appears to have passed its meridian of
> popularity, owing in some measure to the offence given by a proceeding
> which I must consider as selfish in its principle and injurious in its
> consequences. What but to this can I impute. . . the refusal to engage
> Mr. Hummel?—How otherwise can I account for the omission of every
> public-spirited act on the part of the society, and its selfish attention
> to the interests of a few of the individuals of whom it is composed?
> I trust to your impartiality for the insertion of this, and am,
>
> Sir,
Your obedient servant,
An Associate

> [We yield to the appeal of our correspondent, but presume that his
> letter will not remain unanswered. Ed.]

The footnote is not surprising, since the editor, William Ayrton, was one of the "aged members." But the renewed protest actually succeeded: the rule was rescinded that autumn, although its repeal did not result in higher artists' fees.

The collapse of negotiations between Hummel and the Philharmonic probably resulted from both Hummel's misconceptions and the Society's problems. It unfortunately did some damage to his reputation, and even twenty years later, William Gardiner wrote, "I met [Hummel in 1831 or 1833] ; a large fat man, and heard him play at the Philharmonic; but so bent upon getting money, that he would not perform gratuitously, even in that society, where I should have thought the honour sufficient . . . I believe all the composers that I have been acquainted with have been good-natured men, except Hummel." [55]

---

[55] William Gardiner, *Music and Friends; or, Pleasant Recollections of a Dilettante*, (3 vols.; London: Longman, Orme, Brown, and Longman, 1838-1853), I, 163-64; I, 473. According to *Grove's* (3rd ed.), Gardiner (1770-1853), a Leicester stocking manufacturer, "attained some notoriety as a writer on and editor of music." His business trips to the Continent enabled him to get to know the works of Continental composers so well that he probably knew more about Beethoven's music than most English professional musicians. Gardiner edited biographies of Haydn and Mozart, produced editions of church music, and wrote such books as *Music and Friends*, "the utility of which is much impaired by its frequent inaccuracy." (*Ibid.*) Alan Tyson (*The Authentic English Editions of Beethoven*, [London: Faber and Faber, 1963], p. 14), writes, "The distinction of having first introduced [Beethoven's] music to England may well belong to . . .Gardiner, who performed the string trio Op. 3 at Leicester in about the year 1794." It is quite possible that Hummel's music was also brought to England by Gardiner. He pirated selections from a Hummel Mass for vol. 4 of his *Sacred Melodies* collection (1830).

"Honours" are, of course sufficient for him who does not need to earn his living by performing! At any rate, lest Gardiner's remarks lead us prematurely into the future, we shall defer examining the circumstances leading to the performances that he heard.

A trip to London was—luckily—not all business. Posterity has unfortunately consigned most of the social moments to its circular file. What little remains largely concerns the versatile Vincent Novello:

> Mr. Hummel is very sensible to Mr. Novello, having sended him his Edition of the Masse. He would already have called to Mr. Novello, having many Compliments to say him from his friend Mr. Streicher at Vienna; but having been much occupied with the arrangements of his Concert, time has not allowed it till now; but Mr. Hummel will take opportunity so soon as possible to meet Mr. Novello.
>
> I am, Sir,
>
> Your most obed. serv.
>
> Hummel

Monday morning [April 26, 1830][56]

Actually, Novello's edition of the Mass—probably Op. 77 with organ accompaniment—was a piracy, but neither Hummel nor Novello seemed embarrassed about it. The two apparently met again soon thereafter at the home of Lucy Anderson:

> May 13th 1830
> 2 New Cavendish St.
>
> My dear [Mr. Novello],
>
> On Sunday next, Hummel, Sir George Smart, and two or three intimate friends, eat a quiet dinner with us at five o'clock, should you have no previous engagement, and will kindly give us the pleasure of your Company to meet them, we shall be *delighted* to see you—with kind regards from Mr. Anderson
>
> Believe me
>
> Yours very truly
>
> Lucy Anderson[57]

---

[56] Original: Lbm, Add. 11,730, f. 81. "Mr. Streicher" was either Johann Andreas or his son Johann Baptist, Viennese piano manufacturers. Hummel's English certainly left something to be desired, but it should not escape the reader's attention that he was self-educated in all subjects but music. I have reproduced his grammatical and orthographical idiosyncrasies.
[57] *Ibid.*, f. 9

Mary Anne Bacon, translator of the English edition of Hummel's *Piano Method* and daughter of the editor of *The Quarterly Musical Magazine and Review* (Richard MacKenzie Bacon), described what may have been this dinner party:

> I met [Hummel] more than once in London and was amused to see his portly person and simple manners among the artificial habits too often reigning over our musical world. At his first dinner party at Mrs. Anderson's she asked him during the evening to play his Grand Duet for four hands with her; both played most admirably, for Mrs. Anderson had long studied Hummel & played his music in public, and the composer was on his mettle. When it was over Mrs. Anderson fled in tears from the room, and about a quarter of an hour afterwards reappeared with her previously elaborately dressed hair combed straight down like a magdalen and innocent of rouge. As for Hummel he sat down again to the piano & extemporised (in which his power was very great) ending by introducing "God save the Queen" [*sic*!] as coolly as if he was playing from notes so much for *art* and *nature*, in two forms.[58]

To commemorate his meeting with Novello, Hummel wrote a three-part Canon in Novello's autograph album, with the words "by Mr. Novello's sincere friend J.N. Hummel. London, 1st July 1830."[59] A second Canon, whose recipient is unknown, appears to date from the same period and must also have been intended as a token of friendship. Its text is particularly charming in its canonic setting:

Think on your friend
Don't forget your friend
Johann Nepomuck Hummel
Do so, I pray![60]

It is understandable that Hummel himself was involved in most performances of his music during the tour. However, the trip to London also stimulated other performances of his works. Even before Hummel arrived, the well-known English pianist Charles Neate had played the E-major Concerto, Op. 110, at the third Philharmonic concert, March 29. We have already seen that Hummel was present at the next concert of the Society, April 19, when Mme. Stockhausen sang the

---

[58] Miss Bacon's autograph collection, Cu, Add. 6,245, facing f. 71. She wrote this sketch of Hummel to accompany the letter mentioned below, p. 69. Since her collection and commentary have the character of a diary, we may fairly assume that her description is relatively accurate—at least as seen through her eyes. It is certainly not fanciful.

[59] The canon is on f. 59, the resolution, in Hummel's hand, on f. 58'. I am grateful to Novello and Co., Ltd., London, who now own the album, for permission to view it.

[60] Original: Lbm, Add. 32,188, f. 33-34.

scena "Deh, calma" from *Mathilde von Guise*. In light of what we now know about Hummel and the Philharmonic, we can understand *The Athenaeum*'s comments:

> Hummel was present the whole evening, and we hope the economy
> of the directors will not prevent our having the gratification on a
> future occasion of hearing him, at a Concert where his great and
> acknowledged talents would be so well and justly appreciated.

Subscribers, having ultimately missed this gratification, of course, were at least treated to the Septet, Op. 74, played by Mrs. Anderson, with Messrs. Nicholson, Willman, Platt, Moralt, Lindley, and Dragonetti, at the eighth concert (June 14).

Performances of Hummel's music were by no means restricted to major concerts or familiar pieces. At a concert on March 24 (not identified in *The Harmonicon*'s May report) a Hummel Mass was heard; the Offertory *Alma Virgo* had its first British performance at a City Amateur Concert, April 5;[61] and the students of the Royal Academy of Music also climbed on the bandwagon—a concert there, on June 5, included "Concerto, Piano Miss E. Child, Hummel."[62] Last, but hardly least, was Madame Malibran, who, having learned the variations composed for her, was determined to sing them. In addition to performances already cited, she presented the work at Benefits of Signor de Begnis (May 21), Spagnoletti (June 7), and Mr. Oury (June 28).[63]

Five days after appearing at Moscheles' Benefit, *i.e.* on June 6, Hummel announced his "FAREWELL CONCERT" for Monday "morning" (2:00), June 21. The place and price were as always; the "immediate patron" was the Duchess of Clarence. This program projects the atmosphere of the grand recapitulative finale of a comic opera. Vocal performers were Mme. Malibran, Miss Cramer, Signor Lablache, and Signor de Begnis.

> Also the high attraction of Mr. de Bériot, who will perform, with
> Miss E. Bisset, a Rondo Brillant for Harp and Violin. Mr. Hummel
> will introduce, in the course of the Concert, the Grand Septetto in
> D minor; a Rondo Brillant; by particular desire, the favourite Grand
> Sonata for two Piano-fortes by Mozart, with Mr. Moscheles; and an
> extemporaneous performance on the Piano-forte.

Although London was preoccupied with the deteriorating health of King George, the concert was a success. From *The Harmonicon* (July) we learn that

---

61 *The Harmonicon*, May, 1830. The word "amateur" seems to have referred mostly to the audience. According to *The Harmonicon* (April, 1830) two series with this title had been formed for the 1830 season, both meeting at the London Tavern. The one that concerns us was led by violinist Nicholas Mori and pianist Henry Forbes. *The Harmonicon* noted with pleasure that both were flourishing, and in the City, yet, where the most recent concerts had ended in 1823. The same journal reported in June that Forbes, Mori, and Lindley played a Hummel Piano Trio in the season's final concert.

62 *The Times*, June 3, 1830.

63 *The Times*, May 22; *John Bull*, June 6 and 27, 1830.

> Such was the desire to hear [Hummel], as it was likely that no other opportunity would be presented, that the room was filled soon after the opening of the doors. So crowded, indeed, was every part, and so blocked up were the avenues, that though we attended before the performance commenced, we could obtain no admission, therefore have only to state, from the programme, that Mr. Hummel played.... [The same information as in the advertisement then follows.]

The Court Journal (July 3) wrote that the patroness, unable to attend because of the King's illness, summoned Hummel to her home the following Friday

> And bestowed on him substantial marks of her patronage. On that day not the slightest apprehension of immediate danger respecting his late Majesty was entertained by any of the Royal Family. What a change a few short hours made. [64]

That evening King George died, and the Duke and Duchess of Clarence became King William IV and Queen Adelaide—hardly useless contacts for Hummel's future.

Hummel made his final appearance at de Bériot's concert, July 5, and left London five days later. His plan to go to Scotland had come to nothing, but otherwise the three months in England had been well worthwhile. Stopping in Paris on his way home, he found his name in the best repute. During his absence (on April 17, to be precise), the *Institut de France* had elected him a corresponding member of the *Académie des Beaux Arts*, on the nomination of Cherubini (to whom Hummel responded with the dedication of Op. 116).[65] Hummel made his only public appearance in Paris on July 17, at a concert given by the pianist Louise Dumont, the wife of his Parisian publisher, Aristide Farrenc. Despite the hot weather, it drew a "nombreuse société," and the improvisation with which Hummel concluded the concert was the hit of the evening.[66]

This was indeed a special occasion, for the concert announcement said, "Hummel returns to Germany and is going to prepare to make his final journey in the North." The reviewer (*La Revue Musicale*, July 24) went so far as to declare that the next tour would mark Hummel's *complete* retirement. This rumor was further stimulated by *The Musical Gem*, an English gift volume published just before the New Year: Hummel would retire to his native land "in the honorable enjoyment, with his family, of that handsome fortune which his talents and his industry have acquired, and his habitual prudence has secured for the comfort and independence of the remainder of his life." The ever-suspicious mind wonders, however, whether such a report was not purposely circulated to stimulate audiences for the next tour, in just the same way that one often announced several "final concerts."

---

[64] The story was repeated by the Vienna *Allg. mus. Anzeiger*, July 31, 1830, p. 124.

[65] *The Harmonicon*, June 1830; also Cherubini letter to Hummel, November 16, 1830; MH, printed Benyovszky pp. 268-69.

[66] *La Revue Musicale*, VIII (July 17 and 24, 1830). Mme. Farrenc played a Rondo and in the Military Septet, both by Hummel.

In August the pre-farewell tour was over. Hummel was back at home, and a friend inquired, "How did it go? Did the Guineas perform well and turn out in great numbers?"[67] Perhaps the English were justified in fearing that foreigners visited them only to enrich themselves!

---

[67] Letter to Hummel from Adolph Wiele, dated August 20, 1830; MH.

The Tour of 1831

THE FIRST grand farewell tour began on schedule. This time, however, Hummel was due only his usual three-months' leave. Because he could not depart until March 22,[1] he had to compress his activities into less time without making them less profitable. A return to Paris, en route to London, while geographically logical, might therefore have been impractical. German and Austrian journals actually reported that he was bound for London and Paris, but his only verifiable stop in France was at Strasbourg, where he gave a concert (April 9) featuring the A-minor Concerto, a then still-unpublished Rondo (Op. 127?) and an improvisation (which won the usual laurels).[2] He did not arrive in London until April 24, well into the musical season, and because travelling time from Weimar to London was only about ten days, we can assume that he spent extra time in Strasbourg or paused elsewhere. Perhaps he lingered somewhere without performing; in any case, he left us no clues to his activities in this period. *Iris*, whose sources were normally very speedy, reported on May 6 that Hummel was preparing to give his first London concert.

His reputation there had not tarnished in the intervening months; Boosey even felt inspired to reissue the expensive *Piano Method*. In addition to performances of his older works, there was great interest in the music of the previous tour, Opp. 113-118, which had been published in the autumn by Cramer, Addison, and Beale. Mrs. Anderson, for one, played the Military Septet (Op. 114) at a palace concert (March 10), a Benefit, and the Philharmonic; in a program at the Royal Academy of Music, a student performed the Fantasy, Op. 116. Older compositions, such as the A-minor and B-minor Concertos, were also revived. Hummel's vocal music was heard at more festivals: the Gradual "Quod quod in orbe" was performed on the fourth night of the Worcester Music Meeting, September 16, 1830; Mme. Malibran sang her Tyrolean variations on the 30th at the Norwich Festival, where an unidentified selection from the Mass Op. 80 was also on the program.

---

[1] WRa, A9866, f. 71.
[2] See Leipzig, *Allg. mus. Ztg.*, June 15, 1831; *Allg. mus. Anzeiger*, April 21, 1831; *Iris*, April 22, 1831. For the program, Leipzig, *Allg. mus. Ztg.*, September 28, 1831.

Although planning for the 1831 tour had begun many months in advance,[3] the timing of the trip could hardly have been worse. Just when civil disturbances over parliamentary reform were accelerating and could be expected to discourage attendance at concerts, Hummel would have to compete with Paganini for the favors of the troubled upper classes. One needs little ingenuity to predict that the sensation-seeking Londoners would be fascinated by great violinist, who had been preceded by years of gossip about his character and finances.

Only a week after arriving, Hummel made two appearances before select audiences at Court, sponsored by Queen Adelaide. *The Court Journal* (April 30) described these affairs:

> Her Majesty's private Band was in attendance at [St. James's] Palace, on Tuesday evening (April 24), to accompany Mr. Hummel in some of his concerted pieces; and he played also twice extempore in his own unrivalled style. Their Majesties, with their usual condescension and kindness of heart, expressed their satisfaction to the eminent composer, at his return to England. Mr. Hummel performed on the Queen's own piano-forte, made by Erard, which had been removed, for the occasion, from her Majesty's apartments to the Throne-room.
>
> Mr. Hummel attended her Majesty's private Concert again on Thursday, and delighted the Royal Party with a new *Rondo brillant*, accompanied by the Band.

Their sign of satisfaction must have been "solid"—although the hundred-odd snuffboxes in Hummel's legacy suggest that solidity and usefulness (or even resale value) were not always synonymous.

The second of these Court concerts marked the British premiere of the *Rondo Brillant*, published later in England as "Le Retour à Londres" (and on the Continent as "Le Retour de Londres"), Op. 127. But the very privacy of any concert at St. James's happily allowed Hummel to present this Rondo—which actually had been heard in Weimar the previous November—as a genuine novelty at the first of his three 1831 Benefits:

> UNDER the immediate PATRONAGE of Her MAJESTY the QUEEN.— Mr. HUMMEL has the honour to announce to the Nobility, Gentry, and his Friends, that his MORNING CONCERT will take place on Wednesday, the 11th of May, at the Great Concert Room, King's Theatre; to commence at 2 o'clock precisely. Principal vocal performers who have kindly promised their assistance:—Madame Stockhausen, who will sing a new air, composed expressly for her by Mr. Hummel; Madame de Raimbaux, a pupil of Garcia, her first appearance in this country; Mr. Bennett and Mons. Levasseur,

---

[3] When Hummel wrote to Mrs. Anderson, October 1, 1830, informing her that she would be receiving a copy of Op. 114—dedicated to her—he inquired about the progress of plans for him to participate in a festival in Birmingham. Hummel also expressed the hope of seeing her again the next season. (Stargardt Auction Catalogue 574, [Marburg, 1965], item 937.)

> from the Opera at Paris. In the course of the concert Mr. Hummel
> will perform his last grand Concerto in A flat (dedicated to Her
> Majesty); "Mon retour a Londres," a new MS. Rondo, brilliant, with
> orchestral accompaniments, composed expressly for this occasion;
> and an Extemporaneous Performance on the Pianoforte. Full
> particulars will be duly announced. Tickets 10s 6d each, to be had
> of Mr. Hummel, 18, Great Marlborough-street; and at the principal
> music shops. An early application for boxes is requested to be
> made to Mr. Hummel.[4]

The fashionable nature of the personnel was rounded off by the participation (in
all three concerts) of Sir George Smart as conductor. Hummel's program, unlike
the names of his assisting artists, remains shrouded in London's mists: apart from
Mme. de Raimbaux's solo—an aria from Rossini's *Sigismondo*—the remainder of
the compositions have defied identification. The "new air" for Mme.
Stockhausen may have been the one that will turn up on another program later
the same season.

It was a morning with impressive attractions, but it came right in the middle
of Parliamentary elections (Commons having been dissolved on April 22), and
was not reviewed in *The Times*. An announcement regarding their letters-to-the-
editor column suggests that political events were crowding Hummel out of
public notice:

> To correspondents. We see no chance of being able to publish any
> letters for a long time, except such as contain mere matters of fact
> relative to the elections.

Iris, however, reported Hummel's evening briefly to its Berlin readership (July 8):

> London. Hummel, in his concert on May 8, has had a great
> crowd and great applause. English money still rewards German
> diligence richly.

Comforting. Had the date been *Iris'* only error, we could have blithely dismissed
this item as trivial. Unfortunately, everything in it was wrong. *The Court Journal*
(May 14), while remaining ardently Hummelite, subtly gave away the bitter truth
that the concert was far less crowded than *The Times'* letters-to-the-editor column:

> Mr. Hummel's first concert, on Wednesday, was attended by a select
> and fashionable audience; and we make no doubt the second will be
> crowded, as was the case last year, for Mr. Hummel's talent is of that
> extraordinary power which scarcely admits of limit to the desire to
> listen; whilst it is hardly possible to decide which is most fascinating,
> his exquisite playing, or his beautiful composition. The piano forte
> Mr. Hummel selected to play upon, (and which we understand has
> been made by Erard for her Majesty) was well worthy of the great
> pianist, for we never heard before such sweetness and power of tone
> united in one instrument. . . .

---

[4] *The Times*, May 9, 1831.

Discouraging attendance might have kept Hummel from giving a second Benefit, had preparations not already been under way. In a letter written sometime before May 11, Hummel had informed George Anderson (husband of the pianist) that, as there was no competition of a "drawing room" (general assemblage of the nobility at St. James's) on Thursday, May 26, he had reserved the King's Theatre Concert Room for a second Benefit.[5] But alas, Paganini soon announced a concert for May 21. Considering that his ticket prices ranged from 10s. 6d. to one guinea for seats (double Hummel's) and from one and one-half to ten guineas for boxes, many music lovers may have had to forego one of the events. And the cheaper, as we know, is not always the more enticing.

On May 22 Hummel revealed the program of his second concert. Other than an extemporaneous performance, nothing in which he was to participate was new. He would play the Mozart two-piano Sonata (with Moscheles) and, assisted by Mori, Moralt, Lindley, and Dragonetti, perform the Quintet Op. 87, a composition completed thirty years earlier.[6]

Iris' sources now clearly improved in frankness:

> London. . .Paganini is still making a furor; he is now giving his fifth concert in the grand Opera House. Hummel, on the contrary, is doing very poor business. His first Concert was sparsely visited, in the second there were only 119 people, of whom half had free tickets. Nevertheless, he has in mind a third concert.

The Spectator (May 28) was equally vivid:

> On Thursday, HUMMEL had a second concert; which, we are grieved to say, was, like the first, so badly attended, that it would hardly defray his expenses, small, comparatively speaking, as they are. MOZART'S grand duet for two pianofortes was played by HUMMEL and MOSCHELES, in a style of absolute perfection, and was worth many concerts of ordinary materials. But the public requires variety of attraction; and HUMMEL, great as he is, must submit to act on this principle, if he wishes to fill his room.

That Paganini had completely monopolized the attention of London's musical world with his eight public concerts is clear enough. For example, in *The Court Journal's* two issues between Hummel's concerts, Paganini's autobiography occupied two full pages. Furthermore, although *The Times* was so preoccupied with the elections that nothing about Hummel managed to squeeze into its pages, Paganini slipped in comfortably through reviews and letters. Hummel, known in England as a fine pianist and composer and an honest man, was hardly as interesting as Paganini, whose character seemed even more compelling than his performing.

---

5 Cu, Add. 6,245, f. 71. Hummel made the reservation personally.

6 Advertisement, *John Bull*, May 22, 1831. Moscheles was honored, for his friendship and assistance with the dedication of Op. 127.

At least this year Hummel and the Philharmonic came to terms. Meeting on May 8, 1831, directors Sir George Smart, Franz Cramer, Mr. Mountain, and William Dance (in the Chair)

> Resolved that Sir George Smart be authorized to treat with Mr. Hummel, offering him twenty-five guineas for his performance at the 7th Concert. [7]

Hummel, perhaps now more aware of the realities of London, was cooperative this time, accepted the fee (the season's highest, and still ten guineas more than the next highest) and played on May 23. An entry in the minutes of the Directors' meeting of May 23 is interesting in this context:

> Resolved that Sig Paganini be written to inquiring his terms for playing at the 8th Concert.
> Resolved that the Directors have each an Extra Ticket for the 8th Concert.

Although there is no subsequent entry regarding this matter, one can infer Paganini's reply from the fact that he did not perform at the Philharmonic that year or any other.

It is, of course, impossible to imagine what the performance actually sounded like, but the Society's papers at least give us a hint of prevailing conditions. To begin with, soloists were very commonly given short notice of their engagement, although to be sure, visitors such as Hummel were sometimes engaged well in advance. Another normal situation was the provision of only one rehearsal—something that has not changed much today. But it is therefore easy enough to understand why the accompaniments to many Concerti were kept relatively easy; Dragonetti, the star of the Philharmonic, considered rehearsals such a nuisance that he would not attend unless paid extra.[8] The Account Books of the Society also provide some idea of the total effect: the orchestra's normal composition was twenty-eight violins, eight violas, eight cellos, six double-basses; paired flutes, oboes, clarinets, bassoons, and trumpets; four horns, three trombones, piccolo (an extra player), and percussion.

Oddly enough, this was actually not Hummel's Philharmonic debut. *The Athenaeum* (April 30) tells us that at the concert of April 25

> Madame Stockhausen. . .sang a very clever song of Hummel's. It chanced that Mr. Hummel was in the room, and Mr. T. Cooke, the conductor of the evening, with great modesty and good taste, resigned his seat at the pianoforte to him, that he might accompany his own song. We should have liked to have seen even a small portion of Mr. T. Cooke's modesty transferred to Mr. Hummel, for we have frequently been obliged to smile at the monstrous pomposity with which the latter gentleman takes possession, as it were, of an

---

[7] Minutes Book, *op. cit.*
[8] See, *e.g.*, Lbm, Add. 17,838, ff. 318,347 (Dragonetti correspondence).

orchestra, and draws attention on himself when he presides at the pianoforte during one of his own compositions. We respect his great genius as a composer, and admire his talents as a performer; but he should bear in mind the genius and talent by which, at the Philharmonic, at any rate, he is surrounded, and keep his 'madness' a little 'in the background.'[9]

This description, while colorful, does not agree with any other from Hummel's entire career, but it makes sense if seen as a reminder that at least some Londoners still resented Hummel's "refusal" to play with the Philharmonic in 1830. Music lovers also were unused to undivided leadership of an orchestra, since London still observed the archaic practice of having both a pianist and the "concertmaster" conduct. There was also the old matter of English sensitivity about foreigners, which showed itself again in *The Athenaeum* (May 28), when Hummel finally made his long-awaited appearance as a soloist:

Mr. Hummel made his first [*sic!*] appearance at these concerts, and played a Fantasia upon an Indian air ["Oberons Zauberhorn," Op. 116]. As a composition it is inferior to many of this clever composer's works which we have heard; but still it is characteristic, and bears the stamp of his genius. His style of playing is remarkably good, and very elegant; but, for tone and expression, he is as decidedly inferior to John Cramer, as he is superior to every other piano-forte player.

Second to Cramer—and, even within the Philharmonic Society itself, of which he was now an honorary member—Hummel felt the sting of playing "second piano" to Paganini:

The Directors of the Philharmonic Society purpose giving a dinner at the Clarendon Hotel, during the present month, to Paganini; on which occasion Hummel, Ferdinand Ries, and Russian [John] Field, will also be invited; it is intended that the guests shall consist only of members of the Philharmonic body. [10]

Unless a good many Benefits went unadvertised and unreported in 1831, Hummel's misfortune is also evident in his guest appearances. He was present May 6 at Mrs. Anderson's Benefit—when she played his Concerto in A-flat—and at Mme. Dulcken's May 28, but actually participated only in Benefits of the violinist Nicholas Mori, May 16, and the singer J.B. Sale, June 3 (where the audience included Sale's student, Princess Victoria, attending with her mother, the Duchess of Kent). [11]

9 The word "madness" was probably in quotation marks to forestall a libel suit.
10 *The Court Journal*, June 11, 1831.
11 According to reports in *The Harmonicon* and other journals.

By this time Hummel had only two and one-half weeks left to his sabbatical, including the time required for the return to Weimar. He could still gamble on retrieving his earlier success after the convening of the new Parliament drew the *beau monde* back to the capital, but he needed more time. On June 20, Hummel wrote to his superior, Baron von Spiegel, the general manager of the Weimar Court Theater, describing his situation:

> Because of political conditions, the London season is less good than last year; the Reform has preoccupied the heads of the English too much, and because of the dissolution of Parliament in April, the Season was interrupted for nearly 6 weeks; all the Fashionables and others ran to the countryside because of the new elections, and the Grand World has been reassembled again in London only since June 14; tomorrow, the 21st, the King will open the Parliament with a great procession, whereby, strictly speaking, only now will my main business begin; meanwhile I haven't been idle and have composed much and diversely.

Hummel added that he had been invited to play in a large concert at Court, June 29, and asked permission to remain abroad for two more weeks, after which he would travel by way of Rotterdam (not Paris), arriving in Weimar on the 12th, or, at the latest, the 15th of July. Presumably hoping to justify the tardiness of his letter (which would have reached Weimar a week after he should have been home), he also mentioned having appeared in Norwich on June 14.[12] (He had played—at a Mrs. Bridgeman's concert—a concerto, the Rondo Op. 127, an improvisation, and a duet with Mrs. Bridgeman. R.M. Bacon's *Norwich Mercury* said that he was the first distinguished pianist to appear there. His great success provoked an appeal for a subscription to bring Paganini to Norwich!) His request was granted, and his leave extended until the end of July.

He must have anticipated no problems from Weimar, because he advertised his "last concert" for Saturday, June 25, at 2:00. Moscheles wrote in his diary that Hummel, hoping to attract a crowd, had, as a concession to English taste, secured the assistance of the troupe of the Italian opera.[13] The advertisements listed the participants:

> Vocal performers: Madame Stockhausen, Mrs. W. Knyvett, Miss Inverarity, Miss Masson, and Mad. Pasta; Signor Rubini, Mr. Vaughan, Mr. W. Knyvett, Mr. Parry, jun., and Sig. Lablache. Instrumental performers; Violin, Mr. Mori; Violincello, Mr. Lindley; Double Bass, Signor Dragonetti; Flute, Mr. Bohm (first flute to the King of Bavaria); Clarinet, Mr. Willman; Horn, Mr. Puzzi; and Harp, Mr. Labarre. The orchestra will be numerous and complete.

Any more variety and catering to prevailing fashion was hardly possible. The singers included those most praised and revered by Londoners; the instrumentalists were largely members of the Philharmonic. Hummel's own contributions were

---

12 WRa, A9866, ff. 73-74[1]. A note in Spiegel's hand indicates that leave had been extended to the end of July. Printed (without note), Benyovszky, pp. 277-78. Hummel had probably been working on Opp. 120-124.

13 Moscheles I, 231.

"Le Retour à Londres," the A-minor Concerto, and the improvisation.[14] We can only guess the difference between a "numerous and complete" orchestra and the usual orchestra for a Benefit.

The result of all this effort? *The Harmonicon* (July) said that the program was well attended, but was "by no means so full as a composer and performer of such high and undisputed talents had a right to expect." Moscheles, on the other hand, wrote in his diary that Hummel's measures to attract a crowd had proved completely effective.[15] *The Harmonicon*'s comments may therefore be partially interpreted as a veiled attack on the supporters of Paganini.

The nobility then had the rare opportunity to hear the rivals—who, incidentally, were acquainted[16]—in an elegant concert given by the King and Queen at St. James's Palace on June 29.

FIRST PART

> Glee, Spofforth, "Hail Smiling Morn," sung by Messrs. Terrail, Horncastle, Vaughan, and Leete.
>
> Romance, Hummel "Doubt not, Love," sung by Miss Cramer.
>
> Grand Duet, Pianoforte, Hummel, played by Hummel and Mr. Sale.
>
> Recitative and Variations, on Three Airs, composed and performed on One String Only (the Fourth String) by Signor Paganini.
>
> Finale to Cinderella, Rossini. Solo part: Miss Inverarity.

SECOND PART

> An Extemporaneous Performance on the Piano forte by Mr. Hummel.
>
> Aria, Mercadante, "Se m'abbondoni" [?] (*Nitroci*), sung by Miss Masson.
>
> Variations upon the Air "Nel cor più" composed and performed without Orchestral Accompaniments, by Signor Paganini.
>
> Finale to the Second Act of *Oberon*, Weber, with Mrs. Knyvett, Miss Cawse, Mr. Horncastle.[17]

Ordinarily we could expect to unearth nothing further concerning a Court entertainment, but in this case—perhaps because of Paganini's participation—a

---

14 *The Harmonicon*, July 1831. It is interesting to remark on the subject of the Concerto, that Hummel did not carry from Germany music for at least some of his published works. In an undated letter—probably from about the time of this concert—to Cocks and Co., the London publisher, Hummel asked for "an exemplary of my Concerto in A minr. which I am going to play with the Accompaniments." Cocks could hardly refuse him the favor, as their edition was a piracy! (Pn, envelope of Hummel letters in the Music Department, no. 7).

15 Moscheles I, 231.

16 They had collaborated in a concert at Weimar, October 30, 1829.

17 Printed program among the papers of Sir George Smart, Lbm, Add. 41,777, f. 64. A Glee à 5, listed on this program to precede Hummel's improvisation, may have been omitted, for it was not reported in *The Times*, July 1.

few more-or-less unrelated details have survived to give at least some clues about what happened. The concert took place in the palace ballroom, at the east end of which a platform had been erected.[18] According to Sir George Smart, the program lasted two and one half hours—a mere nothing for London—from 20 minutes to ten until a quarter past midnight.[19] The "band" consisted largely of pupils from the Royal Academy of Music, but the leader was Franz Cramer, brother of J.B. Cramer and one of London's most experienced orchestral musicians. Regarding the music, Sir George informs us that Hummel's improvisation incorporated "airs" from Handel's *Judas Maccabeus* (thereby recognizing the English royalty's traditional partiality towards Handel's music). It is quite possible that the Romance was the same unidentified composition sung by Mme. Stockhausen at Hummel's first Benefit. As for the artists, it would of course be interesting to know what sort of compensation they received, and again Sir George, who, as usual, was the contractor, is informative. His records show payments of fifteen guineas each to the Misses Inverarity, Cramer, Masson, and Mrs. Anderson; ten to Miss Cawse; eight guineas to Messrs. Vaughan, Terrail, Horncastle, Leete, Sale, and Sir George himself; and one guinea to the music porter. "Signor Paganini had a present of a Diamond &c. Ring-Value 50 guineas Sir A. Barnard informed me. Mr. Hummel—applied to me for payment— I refer'd him to Sir A. Barnard. Mr. Attwood (who had conducted his own Glee) *not* inserted for Payment by order of Sir A. Barnard." The fees were commensurate with London's norms. Only Hummel's is missing, and all attempts to find it were unavailing—I could not locate Sir Andrew Barnard's account books.[20]

It may also have been Paganini's presence that attracted the press, but surely the King and Queen could hardly have anticipated the trouble that this event would cause. Suddenly they were right in the middle of a journalistic squabble about the obligations of the Royal Family to encourage local talent. Whereas *The Court Journal* (July 2) pointed out that all the vocal performers were English, *The Harmonicon* (September), seeing it from another angle, remarked angrily that of all the compositions, only two were English. For Hummel it was also no triumph. *The Times* (July 1) viewed Paganini as the center of the evening and Hummel as a mere ornament; *The Court Journal* did not even mention our unlucky hero. The prize for English chauvinism, however, goes to *The Morning Chronicle* (June 30),

---

18 *The Court Journal*, July 2, 1831.

19 Lbm, Add. 41,777, ff. 64-64¹.

20 Sir Andrew Francis Barnard (1773-1855), General in the British Army, had been appointed Equerry to George IV in 1828 and, in 1830, was gazetted one of three "commissioners for affixing His Majesty's signature to instruments requiring the same." He was later made Clerk Marshall to Queen Adelaide. (*Dictionary of National Biography*.) An early supporter of the Royal Academy of Music, he was described by Mary Anne Bacon as "passionately fond of Music, which he understood as a science, & pursued with great ardour as an amateur." (Cu, Add. 6,245, opposite letters from Sir Andrew to the Bacon family.) King William's papers, which might have contained Hummel's fee, were destroyed shortly after his death.

which mentioned only Miss Inverarity. Not a word about Hummel *or* Paganini!

Hummel now made a brief tour to the provinces.[21] On July 5 and 7 he played in Manchester's "Gentleman's Subscription" series, with a largely amateur orchestra. In format, these programs did not differ from London's. The first concert included the A-flat Concerto, an improvisation, Overtures by Auber and Winter, and vocal selections; the second, "Le Retour à Londres," the Tyrolean air and variations, sung by Mme. de Raimbaux, an improvisation, Overtures by Auber ("repeated by desire") and Weber, and other vocal music. Hummel's success far surpassed what he had been experiencing in London: more than one thousand persons—nearly a full house—were said to have heard the second concert. The following day—Friday the 8th—after travelling the thirty-six miles to Liverpool, he performed the A-minor Concerto, the Grand Duet Op. 92 (with Mr. Hatton), and extemporized. This concert was filled out with two ballads sung (and perhaps composed) by Mr. Parry jun. "accompanying himself on the harp, with much success," and a violin solo by the conductor from Manchester, a resident Swiss, J.Z. Herrmann. Unfortunately, the program was arranged on short notice and must have had a small audience. Our informant, the correspondent to *The Harmonicon* (August), lamented, "Could he have waited till the following Monday, (Hummel) would have had a most excellent concert, but he was obliged to return immediately to London.

Hummel's affairs were at an end, and he prepared to take leave of England. The day before his departure, he wrote a farewell letter to Sir George Smart. It begins with the usual formalities and then proceeds to a discussion that is reminiscent of the aftermath of the Paris tour of 1825:

London July 16, 1831

My dear Friend,

Leaving London tomorrow morning and having still much to do to get of, I am deprived of the pleasure of taking leave from You personally, therefore excuse me.

I give You my best Thanks for all your Kindness and Friendship You have done to me, and believe that I shall never forget it; and if in any way I can be in something agreeable to you in Germany, I hope You will look at me as your very truly friend who shall execute your wishes with the greatest pleasure.—

My Mathilde de Guise being as for the subject too simple for english Stage, which I find myself knowing now the theatrical taste of this Country, I shall send later another Poëme to Mr. Kemble which certainly will please him better; or if he chuses to select one himself to be composed by me, we shall certainly agree together.—

---

[21] Detailed report in *The Harmonicon*, August 1831 (where the complete programs are printed).

I shall at any time be very glad to receive some Notice from You to
Germany, as I will not fail to do so also if You permit me.
Remember yourself sometimes on Your truly and most sincere friend.

Hummel.[22]

This project for an opera died, probably no later than 1832, when Charles Kemble
left England after years of financial crisis at Covent Garden Theatre, of which he
had been manager. A vague plan (mentioned in *The Athenaeum*, September 10)
for Hummel to superintend and compose several new works for the Dublin Festival
also led to nothing.

Hummel departed on July 17. In return for Queen Adelaide's many kindnesses,
he proposed to take with him any letters that she might wish to be delivered in
Germany, an offer which, although declined, produced a mark of her gratitude
in the form of a silver medal of the King.[23] Hummel travelled speedily and at the
beginning of August was already busy as co-director (with Hippolyte Chelard) of
the second festival of the Thuringian-Saxon Music Union at Erfurt.[24] He must
have been relieved to be in familiar territory, for his tour can only be described as
a failure. *The Spectator*, (July 2) accounted for this sad result by saying that
Hummel had arranged his programs badly. Its critic was firmly convinced that
Hummel was at his best as a composer of vocal music, and that he had few equals
in the field of sacred music. His Masses, *The Spectator* continued, equalled and
often surpassed those of Mozart, and in his D-minor Mass he rivalled Handel as a
"fugist." But rather than presenting such great works, Hummel had chosen to give
concerts "on a level with those of mere Italian benefit-makers." This, to the
newspaper, was a great mistake, for it felt that there were many pianists who could
surpass Hummel in giving to the concert audience of 1831 the kind of sensational
performances that it demanded. What it amounted to was precisely this: could
Hummel compete with the Paganinis, Liszts, and their imitators? *La Revue Musicale*
(August 27) answered the question: "The concerts of M. Hummel were not at all
productive this year; all attention was fixed on Paganini." But Hummel went
down fighting—his new piano fantasy "Recollections of Paganini" shows that he
knew how to capitalize on a loss.

---

[22] Lbm, Add. 41,771, f. 90. On the same day he wrote a short Impromptu for piano,
now preserved in Vienna, Gesellschaft der Musikfreunde, MS. VII. 34000. The Impromptu
was probably written in the album of one Miss Harvey, to whom a piano piece by Moscheles
on the *verso* is inscribed. Hummel's composition is signed "Your friend/J.N. Hummel," and
dated "London 16th July 1831."

[23] Letter to Hummel from Sir John Barton at Windsor Castle, July 14, 1831: MH.
Hummel had probably come to know the Queen even better in 1831 through her sister, the
Duchess Ida of Saxe-Weimar, who was visiting in London during the Spring. The Duchess
had been one of the guests at the Royal Concert, June 29, according to *The Times*, July 1,
1831; she had arrived in London May 18 (*The Court Journal*, May 21, 1831). When
Hummel died, his legacy was crammed with medals.

[24] Hummel conducted his Mass Op. 111, the Offertory "Alma Virgo," and
Haydn's *Creation*.

Intermission

IN 1832 HUMMEL had no important tour. We can assume that the last English trip was discouraging, but there was a greater deterrent—cholera.[1] At first, despite the epidemic, Hummel did not lose hope of at least a short journey. In March he talked of going to Vienna that June, and as late as June 9 wrote his friend Ignaz Castelli, "Perhaps I shall still come to Vienna with my family this year if the road there has been cleansed of Madame Cholera."[2] Yet although the Leipzig *Allgemeine musikalische Zeitung* (June 27) continued to encourage the Viennese hope for a visit by the "Grand Master" of pianists, the trip was finally deferred until 1834. This was a prudent decision, for newspaper reports indicate that the epidemic was keeping audiences at home and theaters empty.

In July Hummel took the cure at Carlsbad, where, on the 25th, he and members of the Weimar Court Theater gave a performance for the benefit of a new hospital. Otherwise, he confined his activities to Weimar, conducting the Court Theater as usual. In October, Moscheles arrived to give some concerts and spent several days visiting with the Hummels, Goethe's widow, and other friends. A letter to *The Harmonicon* (December) described Moscheles' evening at Court, October 25, when Hummel conducted and the "most distinguished nobility" were present:

> During Mr. Moscheles' performance of an extemporaneous fantasia, the Grand Duchess sat on one side of him, and Hummel on the other, the former supplying the artist with the subject on which he was to expatiate. Hummel subsequently gave a grand dinner party, at which many of the principal nobility and the most distinguished artists were present. On this occasion Moscheles and Hummel played extemporaneously on one piano-forte, and the applause they received was correspondent to the extraordinary talent of two such artists.

---

[1] For the situation in London see *The Harmonicon*, March 1832; for Paris, *ibid.*, May, 1832.

[2] En, MS. 594, no. 2101(r).

A four-hands improvisation was certainly a fitting testimonial to the mutual esteem of these great pianists. But Moscheles, busily touring Europe, unfortunately had no time to enjoy this old friendship, and left for Erfurt immediately after dinner. [3]

At the end of the year the Grand Duke added to Hummel's many honors the Weimar Order of the White Falcon.[4] The *Allgemeine musikalische Zeitung*'s report of the ceremony (January 9, 1833) concluded in a most interesting manner:

> At the same time it cannot be a matter of indifference to the friends of genuine pianoforte virtuosity to learn that Hummel intends to make only one more grand concert tour, and indeed to the far north, and with it plans to terminate his public piano performances.

It is immaterial whether or not this announcement was designed to stimulate audiences for the tour. The next trip was indeed to be the northern finale.

---

[3] The evening is also discussed in Moscheles, I, 255.

[4] Diploma dated December 28, 1832, and statutes of the Order: MH.

The Tour of 1833
Hummel the Conductor

THE FAILURE OF HUMMEL'S 1831 TOUR must have suggested that he needed
to try a different approach. And change he did, by returning to London this
time as a conductor. This was not a new trade—he was far from a novice on the
podium—but the true background to his new role in London is a product of the
tangled world of opera there. In the 1830's, Britain's operatic culture was still
overwhelmingly Italianate, as it had been for the previous century. Although
the Covent Garden Theatre had presented a fragment of *Der Freischütz* in
German in 1829, German opera in the original language was virtually non-existent
in England until 1832, when the German singer Joseph August Röckel organized
a company and brought it to The King's Theatre. Röckel was not operating
blindly—he had experienced great success with a similar venture in Paris from
1829 to 1831.[1] On January 14, 1832, *The Athenaeum* revealed Röckel's
prospectus. The repertoire was to consist of *Fidelio* (first time in England),
Euryanthe, Freischütz, Hochzeit der Figaro [sic] , *"Don Juan"*, *"Belmonte e
Costanza"* [*Entführung*] , Spohr's *Jessonda*, Lindpaintner's *Der Vampyr*,
Emmeline by Weigl, *Die Räuberbraut* by Ries, and *Macbeth* by Chelard (who
was to conduct all performances). The impact of these rarities would be
softened by the usual Italian operas.

Despite the good intentions of Monck Mason, the manager of the King's
Theatre, and a record-breaking subscription, the season as a whole was a total
failure—not because German opera was such an incredible novelty, but because
of extravagant productions and dismal performances. Of the German operas
that had been projected, only *Fidelio, Macbeth*, and *"Don Juan"* (in German!)
saw the light of day. To these, an abridged version of Weigl's popular
Schweizerfamilie and, in French, Meyerbeer's *Robert le Diable* had also been
added. Mason lost his entire investment and the lease on the theater was
returned to the former holder, Pierre Laporte. Yet Mason's imaginative risk had
been correct—the German operas, although few in number, had enjoyed real
success in principle. The triumph of the idea (as opposed to the failure of its

---

[1] W. Barclay Squire, "Röckel," in *Grove's*, 3rd ed.

realization) was particularly pronounced, since several earlier attempts to bring French and German opera to London had been rejected by the Lord Chamberlain, the overseer of public theater.[2]

Mason made one last and equally ingenious attempt to recover his lost fortune the following season:

> Mr. Mason, we hear, is anxious to obtain permission to give operas in the months of November and December. This might not prove an unprofitable speculation. Although the fashionable patrons of music are then absent from town, there is a large class of residents to whom the Germans chiefly owe their success, who would certainly give him their willing support. We are, indeed, inclined to think that it would be a very beneficial regulation to give nothing but German operas, up to Easter, when the principal Italian singers having fulfilled their engagements in Italy and at Paris, Mr. Mason might secure a most efficient and complete corps. (*The Athenaeum*, August 11, 1832.)

Mason must have been aiming for the rising commercial class, which was often denied access to the socially-restricted concert world. Predictably, his sailing was stormy. Subscribers to the King's Theatre threatened to fight the scheme—which would have been a real innovation in London's musical life—by withdrawing their support from the more conventional but prestigious Italian opera season. The pressures on the Lord Chamberlain, particularly from the enormously powerful Italian opera interests (many of them aristocrats), were immense, and when he finally denied Mason permission to implement his plan, all seemed lost. *The Athenaeum* (August 25) commented,

> Mr. Mason is thus cruelly prevented from the best chance he had of recovering his lost fortune, and the English public shut out from the most intellectual of musical enjoyments.

The newspaper suggested that Chelard and the German troupe hire a summer theater.

Mason was left high and dry, but the result, for the English public, turned out to be the very opposite of a lost "intellectual musical enjoyment." Chelard arranged to lead his company at another theater, and, according to a report in *The Athenaeum* (December 15),

> Herr Roekel. . . left for Germany on Sunday, authorized by Laporte to make the necessary engagements [for a German troupe at the King's Theatre]. This looks very much like overstocking the market, and will have the effect of dividing a musical audience, not more than sufficient for the support of one company.

By the end of the same month, arrangements were crystallizing:

---

[2] See the monthly reports in *The Harmonicon*, 1832.

Monsieur Chelard, it appears, arrived in London (this week) to
superintend the production of his "Metternacht" at Drury Lane and
to direct the German operas at the same theatre; whilst Gühr, the
most celebrated disciplinarian of Germany, is expected to direct the
rival company at the[King's Theatre]. (*The Athenaeum*, December 29).

The rival companies were now a reality, but when the new prospectus for the
King's Theatre was published in February, 1833, it listed as conductor not Karl
Wilhelm Guhr, conductor of the Frankfurt theater, but Röckel's brother-in-
law, J.N. Hummel.

News of the arrangements spread almost immediately to the Continent, where
London's operatic innovation was eagerly watched. This, after all, could have
signaled the opening of a new market for non-Italian singers. Although Hummel's
name was not mentioned in the initial report (in *Iris*, February 15), by the time it
reached Vienna's *Allgemeiner musikalischer Anzeiger* (March 21), emphasis had
shifted to the conductor and a reported fee of 1000 pounds plus travel expenses.
This was passed along by *La Revue Musicale* (April 20), and *The Harmonicon*
(June). *The Harmonicon*'s skepticism about the fee is understandable, but as the
source of the story was a journal edited by Hummel's close friend Castelli, any
comment as to its veracity is difficult. The amount is a bit improbable, however.

Hummel, accompanied by his wife (Röckel's sister), began his three-month
leave for 1833 late in February. Having placed their children in the care of their
friend Max Seidel, an actor at the Weimar Court Theater, and Hummel's Viennese
publisher Tobias Haslinger, they endured a cold and rough journey, arriving in
snowy London on March 1.[3] On the ninth (Hummel wrote to Baron von Spiegel),

I was called to Windsor by the Queen; I had to try the castle organ
after the afternoon service, and improvise something requiemish in
remembrance of the deceased Princess Luisé (who lies buried there)–
which the King attended;–in the evening I improvised three times
on the Piano Forte in the castle; both of their Majesties are in the
best of health, especially the King, who for a long time was not
so sprightly.[4]

---

[3] Letter to Baron von Spiegel, dated March 23, 1833. Original: WRa, A9866, ff. 96-97;
printed: Benyovszky, pp. 288-89. According to this and another communication from
Hummel to Spiegel, the Grand Duchess had given Hummel a letter to present to the Princess
of Orange in Holland. Assuming that the letter was simply a friendly one of recommendation,
Hummel had not hesitated to change his travel plans between Cologne and London in
accordance with altered ship schedules, going via Calais rather than Rotterdam. Upon arrival
in London he heard from Weimar - to his horror - that the Grand Duchess had been anxiously
awaiting a reply from the Princess. The day was saved thanks to the presence of a member of
the Dutch Court, who took the letter personally to the Princess. Hummel added that his wife
was so worried she was nearly ill; "that I am a better Kapellmeister than a secret Chargé
d'Affair I gladly confess." The second letter is dated April 2. Original: WRa, A9866,
ff. 99-100; excerpts printed in Benyovszky, pp. 290-91.
[4] Letter of March 23, *op. cit.* The princess was Louisa of Saxe-Weimar.

Not that Hummel was so sprightly himself. His cold was followed by an attack of influenza, which he shared with three-quarters of London,[5] but he soon had to begin his main activities. On March 14 the opera season opened with *Der Freischütz*,[6] featuring (according to the advertisements) new scenery, costumes, decorations, and a chorus of fifty. The management doubtless considered a glamorous production a necessity, since the Londoners might be apt to ignore operas that did not display their favorite singers. Indeed, only Henriette Sontag, returning after a four-year absence, had any local reputation. (Hummel's own acquaintance with his singers may have been scarcely more substantial. While he probably knew or knew of some of them through the world of Continental opera, the Weimar Theater Archives show none of them in a major role under Hummel's direction.)[7] The cost of these treats? Admission charges that were even more expensive than usual: two and three guineas for private boxes, 10s. 6d. for stalls, 7s. for public boxes and the pit, and 3s. in the gallery. There was one enticement to compensate for the high prices—nightly *divertissements* starring three of the leading dancers of the period, Marie Sophie Taglioni and Theresa and Fanny Elssler.[8]

---

[5] Letter to Seidel, April 12, 1833. Printed Benyovszky, pp. 286-88.

[6] *Freischütz* was not new to Hummel. Whereas drama at the Weimar Theatre began a decline following Goethe's resignation in 1818, the opera received increasing support, possibly because the Grand Duchess and Hummel were closely associated as student and teacher. New operas, quickly produced at the Theater, included *Der Freischütz*, premiered May 4, 1822 with such success that it had to be immediately repeated 5 times. (Adolf Bartels, *Chronik des Weimarischen Hoftheaters 1817-1907* [Weimar: Böhlaus, 1908] p. XI.)

[7] For example, correspondence in the collection of Maria Hummel shows that Hummel and Nina Sontag's sister Henriette (also a singer) were good friends. I have had limited success identifying the other members of the cast of *Freischütz*. Joseph Binder (Prague, 1792 - Pest, 1845) was engaged at about this time by the Imperial Opera, Vienna (Fétis, *Biographie*); he sang the role of Max. Binder appeared at Weimar in 1836 in the roles of Rodrigo (*Otello*), Florestan, and Zampa (*Die neue Zeitschrift für Musik*, November 29, 1836); reports in Leipzig *Allg. mus. Ztg.* show that he had a substantial reputation throughout the 1820's, especially for performances in Prague. Heinrich Blume (1788-1848) (Caspar), of the Royal *Schauspiel* company in Berlin, was noted for such roles as Don Giovanni (*La Revue Musicale*, May 15, 1830; Fétis, *Biographie*). An evaluation of Blume's ability is found in Berlin *Allg. mus. Ztg.*, June 4, 1828. Less information is available on the others. Mme. Pirscher (Agathe) was a leading singer in the Mannheim Opera in 1835 (Leipzig *Allg. mus. Ztg.*, January 6, 1836); Herr Köckert (Cuno) was from Dresden (*Iris*, February 15, 1833) and had sung at Bremen (Leipzig *Allg. mus. Ztg.*, December 23, 1829) and in concerts in Leipzig as early as 1824 (Berlin *Allg. mus. Ztg.*, December 1, 1824 - a concert given by Moscheles). Herr Ehlers (Killian) may be the one who sang in Spontini's *La Vestale* at Weimar in 1817 (Bartels). I have been unable to identify Hrn. Dolle, Brossin, and Heysel, all advertised as making their first London appearances. Mlle. Nina Sontag was singing the part of Aennchen.

[8] The Elsslers were daughters of Johann Elssler, Haydn's copyist; Hummel may have known them in his Vienna days. *The Times*, March 16, advertised a special performance of one act of *Der Freischütz*, the second act of *Cenerentola* (with Domenico Donzelli), and the ballet *Faust*, for the evening of the 16th. The composer of the *Faust* music is identified as Adolphe Adam in the article "Elssler," *Grove's*, 3rd ed. According to *The Morning Chronicle*, March 18, the illness of a singer forced the last-minute substitution of an act of *La Donna del Lago* for the *Cenerentola* excerpt.

The opening night was well attended by the newspapers, which responded with such diversity that they might easily have seen totally different productions. Happily for our story, they were almost unanimous in calling the orchestral playing under Hummel "excellent." *The Court Journal* (March 16), which was *very* upset about the singers, said, "We cannot speak too highly of the admirable manner in which the gentlemen of the orchestra acquitted themselves; their performance of the overture was masterly, and drew down an enthusiastic *encore*. The whole was admirably conducted by Hummel." Only *The Harmonicon* (April) reacted negatively to Hummel: "Hummel's times (tempi). . . were all quicker than those of the composer, as he gave them at Covent Garden. Which of the two is most likely to be right, we leave our readers to determine." In view of the fact that Weber had last conducted *Freischütz* in London in 1826, the critic deserves our compliments for his memory! Even higher praise goes to *La Revue Musicale* (April 27) for unquestioningly repeating this criticism.

Hummel gave his own assessment of the opening production in a letter to Baron von Spiegel on March 23, two days after the second complete performance:

> The German opera began on the 14th of March with *Freischütz*, and has been received very favorably. *Mad. Pirscher*, a pretty woman with a beautiful voice has really appealed and is the center of attraction here; *Nina Sonntag* did the most that was possible, and was likewise received with applause, while one still recalls her sister Henriette with great pleasure. *Binder* likewise was pleasing; one recognized in him a refined singer, but nevertheless wished for a somewhat stronger voice for the large hall. The tenors have a rather tough situation here this season next to the Italian Donzelli, the most beautiful and strongest voice that exists now; the remainder of the Italian company is less than mediocre; on the 21st the Queen visited Freischütz with a sold-out crowd; the Germans burst out with God Save the King.[9]

Hummel omitted saying that only the presence of the Queen had provided an attraction sufficient to fill the house. *The Spectator*, writing (March 16) of "Laporte's German Campaign," commented that the increase in price had been unwise: because German opera was not yet "a place of fashionable resort," scarcely 100 were in the pit (which had benches for 800!) on the opening night. *The Harmonicon* (April) wondered further why Laporte had not calculated that 100 tickets at seven shillings (*i.e.*, the pit) would be less profitable than 500 at five shillings. "Up to the moment," they said, "the speculation has proved a very losing one, and we do not hear of any new opera being in readiness." All that was announced was one more performance of *Der Freischütz*, on the 28th.

The Harmonicon's information about the repertoire was fairly accurate. While *Iris* (February 15) claimed that the German opera season would include Spohr's

---

[9] Letter of March 23, *op. cit*. As in many other letters, Hummel appears to be scouting for singers for future engagements at Weimar.

Jessonda, Marschner's *Templer*, and Reissiger's *Libella*, such variety was flatly impossible, as Hummel explained to von Spiegel:

> We finally had to finish up with Freischütz at Easter, since for
> several years it has been cranked out too much. Laport [*sic*]
> doesn't want to let us give *Fidelio* for our second opera, although
> it is all ready; we can't present *Euryanthe* at this moment, because
> he has had a falling out with *De Meric*, who should sing *Eglantine*,
> and has just now dismissed her; as a result on Thursday after Easter
> we shall give *Zampa*, which is still quite new here and is already
> known to most of the troupe; thereby we also win some time.—
> In Germany, and at least in Weimar, one has some notion of the
> confusion in the theatrical performances here. It is a truly republican
> administration. One gets to see the impressario scarcely once a week,
> for a few minutes and with half an eye, when one can only with the
> greatest effort extract from him what he really would like and what
> is to be undertaken. I must therefore employ all the energy possible
> to keep the machine in action to some extent; and so it is without
> exception in the theaters here. . . .[10]

Luckily, Laporte finally permitted two performances of *Fidelio*, April 9 and 10, with Mme. Pirscher (Fidelio), Nina Sontag (Marzelline), Blume (Rocco), Binder (Florestan), and Köckert (Pizzaro); both evenings concluded with the Elssler's *Sonnambule divertissement. Fidelio* was already familiar to Londoners through productions in English, and as a result the German troupe had to contend with the supposedly long memories of the natives and their penchant for making comparisons. This time everybody recalled the *Fidelio* production of 1832, with Wilhelmine Schroeder-Devrient in the title role. *The Court Journal* (April 13) felt that the new performance, under Hummel, was better than any in recent years; *La Revue Musicale*'s correspondent said (May 25) that, despite the German troupe's being in better condition than the Italian opera troupe—whose deplorable state was blamed on Laporte—on the whole the Germans did not receive public favor equal to that of the previous year. But Hummel wrote his friend Max Seidel that the two performances went well, with the canon, the prisoners' chorus, and the finale to Act II encored both times.[11]

All in all, *Fidelio* seems to have fared better than *Der Freischütz*, and hopes for a better repertoire soon began to rise. *The Morning Chronicle*, which liked the German series, lent its support (March 18):

> If we are not misinformed, it was Laporte's intention to have given
> German Operas at the King's Theatre twice a week before Easter,
> had he been able to obtain permission, which was refused, on
> account chiefly of the injury that would be done to Drury Lane.
> This decision is just to all parties. After Easter circumstances may

---

[10] Letter of March 23, *op. cit.* Hummel's comments about the management accord completely with those of journalists.
[11] Benyovszky, p. 287.

be different; and the case of Monck Mason [*i.e.*, his failure] is a
precedent in favor of the present lessee of the [King's Theatre].

Hummel described the season thus far and his hopes for the post-Easter period
to Seidel:

> Our houses [for *Freischütz* and *Fidelio*] were still not very
> overflowing, for the fashionable do not return to London before
> Easter and out of old habit do not visit the theater until not earlier
> than 8 - 14 days after Easter. Sunday of next week we give *Zampa*,
> which we have newly rehearsed and here is still totally new; we hope
> it will draw and firm up the box office. Besides, Laporte does
> everything to satisfy the public. The Elslers have gone over less
> well than in Germany; today they dance for the last time; the
> beloved Taglioni appears tomorrow. [12]

Performances of *Zampa* (with Binder in the title role and Mme. Pirscher as
Camille) took place on the 19th and 25th, each time followed by the *Faust*
divertissement. Hummel already knew the opera, having conducted its first
Weimar performance shortly before leaving for England.[13] This production,
however, had the unusual feature of a new finale to Act III composed by
Hummel himself.[14] Both the work as a whole and Hummel's finale provoked
mixed reactions. *The Spectator* and *The Harmonicon* thought that the finale
exhibited Hummel's skill as a dramatic composer and strengthened the opera
(which they did not like); *The Court Journal*, *Iris*, and *La Revue Musicale*, all
of whom liked the opera, thought the finale was well written but felt that the
idea of a new finale was in bad taste. *The Spectator*'s comment accorded with
its earlier opinion of Hummel as a vocal composer:

> We have been anxiously expecting the production of some novelty
> in this department of the King's Theatre, and at length the *Zampa*
> of HEROLD made its appearance. Under the direction of such a
> man as HUMMEL, something better might have been expected; and
> we marvel that he had not the vanity enough to produce his own
> *Matilda*, in place of an opera little known in this country. [*Zampa*]
> is tedious and dull. . . the music is neither very good or very bad. . . .
> The finale to the third act was rewritten by HUMMEL, and is the best
> thing in the opera.

May Hummel have savored this compliment, for by now his mood must have
been truly foul. The Drury Lane revival of *Fidelio* (in English, with Schroeder-
Devrient) had spread the audience so hopelessly thin that all wishes for novelty

---

[12] *Ibid.*

[13] Theater poster in WR.

[14] As the finale by Hummel is not mentioned on the program for the Weimar performance,
which ordinarily gives such details, it seems fair to assume that it was composed especially for
London. This finale is one of the few known unpublished compositions by Hummel to have
disappeared without a trace.

were in vain.[15] The Laporte-Hummel company gave only two more performances (of *Der Freischütz*, on May 15 and 16), the second of which was a benefit for the principal performers.

On the whole, then, the German opera troupe brought to London by Röckel for Laporte had been unable to repeat the success of the previous year. The English musical public was still too overwhelmingly composed of the "fashionable" to provide reliable support for unfashionable German operas. Moreover, the existence of a second company at Drury Lane had insured the further dispersal of the true music lovers who could have made a season rewarding for *one* company. The distressing outcome of Laporte's speculation was not a good omen for the remainder of Hummel's trip.

Again the Virtuoso

With the opera behind him, Hummel turned to his usual work as a composer-virtuoso. If the fate of the opera company depressed him, the popularity of his music since 1831 ought to have been encouraging. For example, in 1832, five of the fourteen Benefits discussed in *The Harmonicon*'s annual report (July) included instrumental works;[16] Hummel was represented on three of them, as follows: Mrs. Anderson played a *Rondo brillant* at her Benefit, May 11; she also participated in one of the Septets (probably Op. 114) at the Stockhausens', June 15; and a group including Mendelssohn performed the Septet Op. 74 at Mr. Sedlatzek's, May 21. The 1833 season also saw important performances of his works. Philharmonic subscribers heard his E-major Piano Concerto (Op. 110), but the pleasure it gave was not unanimous:

> . . . it was especially bad taste to allow MR. WRIGHT to perform one of Hummel's Pianoforte Concertos on the Harp; and that, too, in the presence of the author. These tricks may do at benefit concerts, but *here* it ought to be a principle, that classical compositions *only* should be performed, and performed in an unmutilated state. Why, above all, should this rule be violated in favour of Mr. T. WRIGHT?[17]

Other compositions by Hummel were heard that year at Mme. Dulcken's Benefit, May 1, at the Royal Academy of Music, and all of these performances, in the traditional London surroundings, followed the old familiar pattern. More significantly, in that same two-year period, Hummel's sacred music became

---

[15] *Fidelio* opened May 4. The company later moved to Covent Garden and produced *The Magic Flute*.

[16] Excluding Moscheles's and Cramer's, which contained almost exclusively their own music.

[17] *The Spectator*, May 4, 1833. Others in the audience for this concert, April 29, were Pixis, Chelard, Mendelssohn, Herz, Bellini. Wright performed it again on May 3 for the annual New Musical Fund Benefit, about which Sir George Smart noted on his program that the Band would not rehearse it, as the principals had just played it. He also says the slow movement was omitted. (Program: Lbm.)

better known, particularly as the number of vocal groups began to increase. One of these additions to London's musical life, the "Vocal Society," was formed in 1833, avowedly to advance the "proper performance" of English music. They did not, however, exclude foreign compositions from their programs, and at their first, third, and sixth concerts—January 7, February 4, and March 18—the Society sang Hummel's Offertory *Alma Virgo*, the *Gloria* from his Mass Op. 77, and excerpts from the Mass Op. 80. Other movements from Op. 80 (and a movement from a Piano Concerto) were performed on the Royal Academy's first 1833 concert. Furthermore, a letter to Vincent Novello from William Aspull, leader of a Nottingham Choral Society, indicates that the reputation of Hummel's sacred music was also reaching that growing city.[18] Looking back, we see that the new vogue of sacred choral music was working in Hummel's favor even as his reputation as a virtuoso was being eclipsed.

It was therefore with at least some of his music reasonably fresh in local ears that Hummel announced his "only morning concert" for May 13, at the Concert Room, King's Theatre. He appears to have spared nothing in the attempt to draw a crowd. *The Times'* advertisement (May 6) stated,

> The most distinguished foreign singers and the celebrated German vocalists (*i.e.*, the opera company) will attend to this concert. Her Majesty has been graciously pleased to permit her private band to attend on this occasion, and the noble Directors of the Royal Academy of Music have also kindly allowed several members of that Institution to assist. Mr. Hummel will perform, for the first time, a new MS. concerto on the pianoforte, composed by him for this occasion; "Le Retour à Londres," a grand MS. Rondo brillante; and an extemporaneous performance.

The announcement in *John Bull* the following Sunday gave some additional details:

> Principal Singers—Madame Pasta, Madame de Meric, Madame Pirscher, Mlle. Nina Sontag, Signor Donzelli, Signor Tamburini, Hr Binder and Hr Blume . . . .The celebrated German vocalists from the King's Theatre will sing—a Song of the Robbers, from Schiller's Tragedy of that name; the Chorus of Priests, from Mozart's "Zauberflote"; the favourite Jaeger Chorus, from Weber's "Euryanthe"; and Messrs. C. and F. Otto, Busse and Gloh (just arrived in this country) will sing two Vocal Quartetts. Tickets, Half-a-Guinea each. . . .

The conductor was again Sir George Smart;[19] the Concerto was the one in F major (published posthumously).

Sadly, all these elaborate preparations were of no avail. Only *The Harmonicon* (July) took any notice of the concert, and although it was complimentary to

---

[18] Dated April 28, 1832; Lbm, Add. 11,730, f. 18. William Aspull was the brother of the prodigy pianist George Aspull.

[19] Lbm, Add. 41,772, f. 82.

Hummel—but not to the German vocalists—it pointed out that "the room was not fully attended." The critic of *The Athenaeum* (June 1) complained sympathetically that there were simply too many Benefits, by "every miserable pianist, flutist, guitarist, singing-master, and singing-mistress. . . . Will it be believed that the two least profitable concerts this season have been given by Hummel and Moscheles, who, in addition to their superior performances, produced for the occasion MS. compositions of high merit!"

The fullest description of this disaster came from the Continent, however, in a "Letter from England" in the second issue (April 7, 1834) of *Die Neue Zeitschrift für Musik*. Although in reading it one must consider the newborn *NZM*'s propensity for exaggerated attacks on the musical establishment, this German account certainly contains at least a germ of truth. The writer—"D.G."— tells of being met on arrival in London by his friend "Franz O."—probably Franz Otto, a participant in Hummel's concert—and being informed by him, "In England Art exists solely as Fashion, and music is an article, spoilt goods. . . every German musician should bring along his bread basket, so that he can live. . . the kid with a bagpipe under his arm makes as much of a furor as Hummel. . ." The author ("D.G."), following Franz O's advice to go to Hummel's concert and see for himself, wrote:

> The concert had been announced eight weeks ago,[20] a very short time to be known, for London. In many music shops there hung the large announcement posters—not unlike the yard-long ones of the [Leipzig] Fair companies—and on them one discovered the names of the co-performers: Mrs. Pasta, Schroeder-Devrient, Cinti-Damoreau, Pirscher, Sontag, Mr. Donzelli, Binder, Blum, Fr. and C. Otto, and the whole chorus of the German Opera under his direction.
>
> There were no fewer than *twenty* different pieces performed; a gay cloth, which Germany's, France's, Italy's, and Respect!—England's composers adorned. An overture began it, performed by the private orchestra of the Queen, whose assistance Hummel had got as a special favor.
>
> Now Hummel played a new concerto in F major, whose aesthetic worth resembles his current compositions; only the Rondo could rather call to mind his earlier time of magnificence. Spirit, life, execution, remained lost to the audience—one saw it on all the faces— they raised themselves up from their seats, watched the beautiful playing of the fingers, wondered at it, and as the double trills now began—everybody slogged away with hands, feet, and canes, as if the lightly-built auditorium were celebrating its own destruction! Don't be so astonished at such applause—the Englishman loves these massive demonstrations.

Madame Pasta's voice (he continued in the next issue) was splendid. But,

---

[20] Probably an exaggeration.

As much as the Beautiful and the Classic were created, so much did the Northern Ice remain cold, until, through the drunken church-raising scene by M. v. Weber, which was arranged for orchestra, solo voice, and chorus, and performed by Herr Blume, it melted quite completely. One saw that here the real element of the Select Society was touched; here everything was comprehensible, one could penetrate into the spirit of the composer—and as now yet another clucking and cackling poultry yard with cow-lowing followed the pigs' grunts, there was no end to the Da Capo clatter, and everyone was delighted right up into their souls. For some time I stood really as if rooted fast, and didn't know if I was in a concert hall at Nukahiwa or in a European capital! Hummel, who through his multiple visits had already got used to this treat, and had paid dearly for his knowledge of this bad taste, declared to me that the Englishman would never reach any higher level of cultivation in the art of music; he could not be blamed for this. The public certainly vindicated him.

For German artists I would like at this point to add an observation that everyone who thinks of making an artistic visit to the British capital ought to consider. Reputation, the highest artistic training, recommendations—even the best ones—do not help one succeed. The example of my friend Knoop from Meiningen proves it. He, who came here on the command of the Queen, couldn't undertake a public concert without losing several hundred pounds. He had already played at Court fourteen times, and had never received any notice from a public paper, for the simple reason that he was too honourable to hire a eulogizer in the newspapers! [Henri] Herz, who only played at Court once, was trumpeted forth in every newspaper; he, however, had paid off quite enough quills. His activities belong under the rubric of *peddler*.

Hummel would have suffered a considerable loss if all of the participating personnel had not relinquished all honoria out of pure friendship for him.

No allowances for journalist prejudice can obscure the obvious loss of support that Hummel was experiencing. The same trend also is evident in his dealings with the Philharmonic in 1833. The Society began with a generous gesture at the Directors' meeting of March 10 (attended by William Ayrton, J.B. and Franz Cramer, Sir G. Smart, and William Dance): "Resolved that a free admission for the Season be presented to Mr. Hummel."[21] Hummel, as we have seen, availed himself of the offer at least once. Then, at the Directors' meeting on May 15,

> Sir George Smart communicates a Message from Mr. Hummel requesting to know whether he was expected to play at either of the remaining Concerts.

---

[21] Minutes Book, *op. cit.* At the meeting were William Ayrton (editor of *The Harmonicon*), Franz and J.B. Cramer, Sir George Smart, and, in the Chair, William Dance. At the meeting of April 27, a similar resolution awarded free tickets to Paganini, Bellini, and Herz. A free admission was also valid for rehearsals.

Resolved that he be informed in consequence of the arrangements for the last two Concerts having been concluded the Directors report they cannot avail themselves of his offer.[22]

Their communication to Hummel was, by English standards, uncivilly abrupt:

Sir, The Directors of the [Philharmonic Society] desire me to [acquaint] you that the arrangements for the remain[ing] Concerts of the Season having been already made, they report that they cannot avail themselves of your assistance.

> I remain Sir
> Your Obd. St.
> W. Watts
> sec.

May 17

The "Associate" of *The Harmonicon* letters of 1830 could have argued that the Philharmonic might well have rejected a man of Hummel's stature more gently and in person, especially as he had been reduced to requesting an engagement. But again there is more than meets the first eye. Four days later, the Society wrote to him,

Sir, I am desired by the D[irectors] of the P.S. [Philharmonic Society] to say that they shd. feel particularly gratified by [your] assistance at the Concert of Monday next provided you can consider them as Artists and be induced to accept the Terms they pay Mr. DeBeriot, and which they have not exceeded to any other performer during the season, namely fifteen guineas.
The favour of an immediate answer will much obbl.

> Sir, Your Obedt Svt
> W. Watts Sec.

May 21

We do not know if Hummel was insulted, and perhaps he was aware that soloists were often hired on short notice. In any event, he did not stand on ceremony:

Sir,

In Answer to Your Kind letter from yesterday I have the pleasure to say, that, in regard to the Honbl. Society of Artists, I shall accept to play *next Monday* at the Philharmonic Society upon the terms of fifteen Guineas they proposed.

---

[22] Minutes Book, *op. cit.* Attending: Mountain, Cooke, Ayrton, Smart. It should be borne in mind that the abbreviated style of the subsequent document may result from the fact that the documents survive as brief minutes-book entries or as rapidly executed copies of outgoing letters.

I shall perform the New M.S. Concerto; and beg you only to
arrange it, that I can be *placed in the first part*, if possible, and that
I may try it on Saturday between 12 & 2 O'Clock, having later several
important businesses.

I remain, Sir,

Your Obedt. Servant
Chevr. Hummel[23]

Why did the Philharmonic Directors change their minds? The minutes-book
suggests that the second communication may have resulted from the sudden
cancellation of performances of new works by Vincent Novello and Sir Henry
Bishop. That change had been announced at that same meeting of May 15,
however. Surely the Directors could have engaged Hummel at once. It therefore
seems quite likely that the Directors, who certainly were aware of Hummel's
dismal season, counted on a bit of humiliation to induce his acceptance of their
terms. At least their statement about the scale of fees was truthful.[24]

One wonders if Hummel knew about the backstage maneuvering. Let us hope
not, for the poor state of his affairs needed no further illustration. Hummel
played in only one of the season's many Benefits. Ironically, it was given (on
June 14) by J.B. Cramer, with whom he had declined to appear in 1830. Five
years after the event, *The Musical World* (February 16, 1838) described their
performance of J.S. Bach's Fantasia in F-minor (arranged for piano four-hands):

Our readers may probably recollect the composition from the
circumstance which attended its production, when performed by
J.B. Cramer and M. Hummel on his last visit to the metropolis, on
which occasion, from a singular fit of nervous feeling, the latter
became completely deprived of the command over his instrument.

In addition to his few public appearances, Hummel also occupied himself in
fulfilling a commission, a Cantata for voices, piano, and harp, to a horrendous
patriotic text by a certain "Lady of Dunstaffnage." This "Orphan's Ode to the

---

[23] Original: Lbm, Loan 48.13 (17), f. 84. The Concerto was the one in F major. Foster
(p. 123) was incorrect in saying that it had been composed for this concert. Not only had
Hummel already played it at his own Benefit—he would hardly have so impoliticly spoiled a
grand premiere of a specially-composed piece—but, as we have seen, it very nearly was never
heard at all at the Philharmonic.

[24] In 1833, Hummel, Cramer, and De Bériot each received fifteen guineas; the singer
Mrs. Wood, £15; Moscheles and singers Mrs. Knyvett, Braham, Rubini, and Tamburini, ten
guineas; all others, five guineas. Hummel's fee of twenty-five guineas in 1831 remained the
highest paid any instrumental soloist until the account books cease in the 1860's. Although
orchestral pay remained constant until 1842, that to soloists generally declined. From 1834
until 1840, fifteen guineas remained the highest fee, and was paid only to Cramer (1834 and
1840), De Bériot (1834), Thalberg (1837), and Theodor Döhler (1838; but he was reduced to
ten guineas in 1839). Liszt, in 1841, received a mere five guineas, although the previous year
he was given a "piece of plate" (silver) for two performances, as was Thalberg in 1836 and
Ole Bull for one performance in 1840. (Data from Philharmonic Account Book.)

Patriots" actually achieved the sizable subscription of over 300 copies, mostly from nobles—and twelve ladies' schools—throughout the Kingdom, but it was hardly in a class with the operatic project discussed several years earlier.[25]

In June, 1834, the Supplement to Ayrton's *The Musical Library* (successor to the recently deceased *Harmonicon*) offered the blackest summary of the 1833 tour:

> Last year [Hummel] once more returned, but the attraction of novelty was much diminished; and the parsimonious manner in which he got up his concerts offering no temptation to the public, his room was deserted and his stay of short duration.

It was a curious situation. Through unusual twists of fashion, *Die neue Zeitschrift für Musik*, a journal that generally sought to make its reputation as an arch anti-establishment organ, had sided with the "Establishment" Hummel against London's dismal public taste; at the same time, *The Musical Library*, a rather typical voice of London's Establishment, effectively sided with an even lower level of vested interests—the truly commercial—against a figure who had come to represent the best in conservative continuity. No allowances for rhetoric can disguise the fact that it was a far cry from Hummel's 1830 glories.

Soon after Cramer's Benefit, Hummel and his wife left England for the last time. He notified his brother-in-law, Röckel, "that they arrived safe but sea-sick in Ostende on June 16, spending until midnight looking for lodging because all hotels were booked." They passed through Brussels, and by the 22nd they were already in Eisenach and the next day, at 4:00 A.M., reached Weimar. Hummel was immediately off to a birthday celebration for the Grand Duke's heir. It was business as usual. The tours to the North were over.[26]

---

[25] Copy: Lbm, H.1690(49). The author of the text used a pseudonym; her real name, supplied by the entry at Stationers' Hall and a letter from Hummel to Röckel (Benyovszky, p. 293) was Anna Harrah McColl. I could not identify her further. On the copy cited, Hummel's and Herz's names have been added to the subscribers' list in pen. On p. 4 is a warning to potential subscribers to be sure to verify the identity of the person soliciting subscriptions, in view of "an audacious, and extensive fraud" in the publisher's name, in Scotland. *The Harmonicon* (September, 1833) called the text "an abominable *mésalliance* of religion and politics. . . the music, by Hummel, and in his best manner, is worthy of so much of the poetry as is borrowed from the inspired writer [Isaiah], and far too good for the uninspired verses that follow. The promoters of this work, however, it seems, intend to make some provision for two orphans out of the proceeds, and we hope that success will attend their benevolent endeavours; wishing at the same time that they had been as fortunate in their choice of words as in their music and number of subscribers."

[26] Letter to Röckel, *op. cit. ante.* Hummel did not lose contact with England. In March, 1835 the two sons of J.A. Röckel arrived in London after completing their studies in Weimar. They were armed with a letter of recommendation from Hummel to Sir George Smart, but there is no evidence that Smart was able to assist with the desired Philharmonic engagement. Hummel's elder son, Eduard, a pianist, came to England in 1838, but had no immediate success.

Postlude

JOHANN NEPOMUK HUMMEL HAD LEFT ENGLAND for the last time. Upon looking back one appreciates what an enormous amount of energy he had devoted to that chilly climate. Indeed, Hummel's final years would probably have been very different without England to stimulate his work. The facts suggest that otherwise he might have virtually retired. His energy was so depleted by poor health that in his twilight years, according to the obituary in *Die neue Zeitschrift für Musik*, Hummel "already had to suspend his functions as Kapellmeister repeatedly." [1] But even before the decline in his vigor, he showed signs of having been artistically stifled, perhaps because of his comfortable life in Weimar, with the house and garden that he so thoroughly enjoyed. In 1860, Liszt, explaining why he was choosing to resign from his own Weimar position, gave Grand Duke Carl Alexander his analysis of Hummel's fate:

> What was the success of the system of *status quo* in the case of
> Hummel, most certainly a highly gifted artist? That one made him
> into a machine, deadened him, and debased him in the artistic world,
> where his activities as Kapellmeister were worth as much as nothing.
> Weimar morally castrated him—and what profit did Weimar get from
> it? I don't envy his lot, and will not arrange my career on the model
> of his, even if I should be proud to create works that resemble his,
> above all those which he wrote before he fell apart here, worn out.[2]

Liszt's conviction that Weimar destroyed Hummel must certainly be interpreted as a sign of his own bitterness. But in a curious way, Hummel substantiated it through his silence: nowhere in his sizable extant correspondence did Hummel complain about his situation. On the contrary, he appreciated the scarcity of positions that combined stability with so many months of freedom to pursue a career as a pianist. Rather than leave the security of Weimar, where he was able to handle local politics to his own advantage, he had even turned

---

[1] *Die neue Zeitschrift für Musik*, November 17, 1837.
[2] Peter Raabe, *Franz Liszt*, (2 vols.; Stuttgart: Cotta, 1931) I, 131. The letter is dated February 6, 1860.

down an offer to direct the Dresden Opera after Weber's death.[3]

The decline in Hummel's activity extended to his work as a pianist and composer. Whereas he had composed prolifically as a young man, during the 1820's the only major project that could sustain his enthusiasm was the *Piano Method*. In his Viennese days he had produced *Singspiele*, operas, chamber music, piano music, and dances of all varieties; now even the prestige-laden opera for Paris died in infancy. Composing, it seems, took second place to teaching and to making arrangements of orchestral masterpieces by Haydn, Mozart, Rossini, and others.[4] But one area of active music-making was increasing during this time: conducting. When we recall that Hummel rarely played works by other composers— probably because his pianistic skill was so closely bound together with his compositional style[5]—we realize that the shifts from composing to arranging and from playing to conducting were both symptomatic of a new-found interest in the music of others.

Perhaps Hummel had become convinced that he was a figure of the past. While at the height of his career he had been sensitive to adverse criticism, even from so ardent an admirer as the conservative *Allgemeine musikalische Zeitung.*[6]

---

[3] Letter to Mosel, June 15, 1827. Original: Wn, Hs. 126/66-7; printed Benyovszky, p. 273. The appointment had already been announced (in the form of rumors) in *La Revue Musicale* (May, 1827) the Leipzig *Allg. mus. Ztg.*, (May 2, 1827), and *The Harmonicon* (August, 1827). Hummel also told Mosel that Weimar had agreed to duplicate all the terms of the Dresden contract.

[4] The arrangements for piano with the accompaniment of flute, violin, and cello. See this author's list in *Notes*, June, 1974, pp. 750-52.

[5] It can hardly be coincidental that his finest compositions come from the time of his greatest activity as a performing pianist.

[6] The Leipzig *Allg. mus. Ztg.*, (September 30, 1824) incurred Hummel's wrath with its review of his *Amusements*, Op. 105, which spoke of much of the set as rather ordinary, and of a few passages as not the sort the critic would want to have on his conscience. Hummel was so incensed that he wrote his publisher Peters (October 16), "I cannot concede that the tottering artistic world shall be led astray by such asses. For this reason, if you please, see to the insertion of the enclosed very moderately written comment in the Musical Newspaper [*Allg. mus. Ztg.*]." The "comment" is lost, and Peters must have cautioned more moderation, for Hummel's next letter (November 9) begins, "In order to show Herr Härtel [the publisher of *Allg. mus. Ztg.*] that I laugh at such assininity, I will be quiet *this time*. But tell him: 'as far as he does not take care that this sort of miserable review, worthy only of a schoolboy, does not appear any longer in his journal, I would, in conjunction with several of my *Accredited Colleagues*, publicly demonstrate to the world what's going on in today's world of reviewing (and particularly this rabble), so that it will no longer be led astray and get cockeyed and false notions about the art, which has been the case for such a long time.' Herr Härtel may then decide whether the *stinging hero of the pen* alone suffices as reviewer for a musical newspaper, or whether he would have to know a bit more than to scribble all over the pages.* I hope that Herr Härtel will keep this in mind for the future, and keep totally silent about me in his newspaper rather than allow such miserable rubbish to be accepted.

*"If it must be, even we in Weimar still know how to wield a good pen." [Originals: Leipzig, State Archive.]

How much more stinging must have been the attacks by the organ of the younger generation, Schumann's *Neue Zeitschrift*? To these increasingly influential progressives, tact was rarely the primary concern. Witness their comments about Hummel's concert in Dresden on April 3, 1834:

> Hummel should make no further concert tour, at least not in Germany and France, where piano playing has reached the pinnacle of culture and only the most extraordinary can please. He significantly debases his well-earned fame thereby. His palmy days are long gone. His art has declined, as his years have increased.[7]

Schumann's own comments about Hummel's Etudes Op. 125 were similar in tone: the Etudes had come too late—they met the needs of a bygone age.[8] Furthermore, there could be no comfort in rationalizing that the Schumann circle was flatly opposed to the style of the old guard, for they were quite prepared to describe Hummel's recently-published Mass Op. 111 as "a really solid work, deeply thought out, nobly and freely treated, full of magnificent ideas."[9] Even this success, however, was only another reminder that his greatest days were over: the Mass had been composed nearly thirty years before.

Weimar did not destroy Hummel. It merely blunted his will to fight. He was truly a figure from the eighteenth century, and could not shake off the overwhelming influence of his childhood teacher and friend, Mozart. Incapable of adapting to a new world, increasingly isolated from the younger generation at home, Hummel for a while had found his refuge abroad. There the demand for the music of the "classical" masters was still stronger than the drive to cast off tradition, and he could flourish among the vestiges of his old world. But there too, the present, with all its excesses of taste, finally arrived to doom Hummel's attempts to stretch the days of his bygone Vienna.

At least a happy, if largely posthumous, ending awaited Hummel in England and France. His mixed success in Paris and ultimate failure in England turned out to be interludes that did not portend the irrevocable downfall of his reputation. In Paris, over the subsequent decades, he was honored as the last great product of Vienna. His compositions retained a place in the repertoire of the amateur French pianist seeking "good taste," and of professionals needing to create a name for virtuosity. In some Parisian circles, the failure of Hummel's second and third trips across the Channel was regarded as an indication of the miserable ears of the English and as an insult to the great pianist that would not be soon forgiven. Fétis, who clearly blamed the Londoners and not Hummel, may have been expressing the opinion prevalent on the Continent when he wrote

---

[7] *Die neue Zeitschrift für Musik*, May 5, 1834.

[8] *Ibid.*, June 5, 1834. The Leipzig *Allg. mus. Ztg.* responded in their review of the Etudes that the Romantics had one trouble: anything which did not belong to the Romantic school was automatically bad to them. (March 11, 1835)

[9] *Die neue Zeitschrift für Musik*, June 30, 1835.

that "the glorious renown of the artist ran aground faced with the indifference of the public of [London], and his sojourn was hardly noticed there."[10] A "private letter" to *La Gazette Musicale*, July 26, 1835, regarding Cramer's departure from England the same year, substantiates Fétis' view:

> The loss of Cramer will be felt profoundly in the epoch in which we live. Despite his efforts and those of his friend Mr. Moscheles to sustain the cause of good music, a false and vicious taste makes rapid progress every day in England. In our fashionable circles, one neglects the works of Mozard [*sic*], Beethoven, Hummel, Cramer, and Moscheles. The noble and beautiful simplicity of these composers is scorned, and nothing can inspire a vogue, if it isn't the empty noise, the false glitter, and the vacuous difficulties that distinguish the New School of Germany and France. At the moment the compositions of Herz, above all, create a furor.

It would be difficult to argue that such reports represent anti-British prejudice in France and Germany rather than a real situation in England (even given Fétis' long-standing distaste for music in London), for England itself was becoming increasingly aware of its own musical failings. The later 1830's witnessed rising standards and greater seriousness on many fronts, as the traditional influence of wealthy amateurs and cliques came under heavy attack. Programs mixing popular songs and opera arias with symphonic music began to disappear, and a nascent tendency to revere the "classics" was strongly encouraged. In these musically literate circles, "learnedness," an asset in the 1820's but a liability during Hummel's last two tours, was again admired. A vivid example of how this change affected Hummel's name is found in two comments about his *Piano Method*. Presenting the older point of view, George Hogarth wrote in his *Musical History* (1835):

> A few years ago, Hummel published a great work of studies for the piano-forte, which must have cost him years of labour, and must be of infinite value to those who have resolution enough to get through it. But its ponderous bulk, and mass of contents, afford a prospect somewhat similar to that of a journey through the Arabian desert, and are sufficient to terrify any one who has not the dogged perseverance of a German student.[11]

Representing the youthful seriousness is a new and rebellious journal, *The Musical World*, which wrote, on January 5, 1838 (two and one-half months after Hummel's death):

---

[10] Article "Hummel," *Biographie Universelle.* The article also appeared in *Revue et Gazette Musicale*, August 8, 1839. Fétis felt that had Hummel not had the misfortune of being a contemporary of Beethoven, he would be remembered as the first composer of his generation.

[11] George Hogarth, *Musical History, Biography, and Criticism. Being a General Survey of Music, from the Earliest Period to the Present Time* (London: Parker, 1835), pp. 373-74.

Hummel. . . has shown in his invaluable studio that there is no achieving great efforts without attention to small ones. If he had not acquired the prodigious mass of information, which is to be found in this legacy to rising artists, he never would have risen to the eminence he enjoyed. But it was not the least distinguishing feature of his genius, that he was able and willing to communicate it so unreservedly and in so perspicuous a manner.

The Musical World soon became one of the most ardent defenders of the man who had so recently been subject to humiliation by the lovers of the "new." The description of the 1831 tour in their obituary of Hummel (October 27, 1837) is characteristic:

About the period of his second appearance here, the style of Herz had become fashionable, while that of Mozart's pupil was voted 'passé.' People streamed out from his concert, while he was extemporising with consummate mastery and elegance. The musicians, however, and those who had formed their tastes upon the highest school in the art, all upheld him with enthusiasm.

In the late 1830's, then, amidst the attempt to educate the English musical public to higher standards, Hummel's name in England recovered its lost status. Victoria's reign cast him as the great pedagogue of his instrument, a savior of modern sacred music, [12] and, above all, a "classic" of his time.

---

[12] *E.g.*, five sacred works were performed in the four Antient Concerts between April 17 and May 15, 1839; Queen Victoria wrote in her diary that of the program of the Antient Concert, May 29, 1844, she had particularly liked the Hummel Motet.

Chronological List of Compositions
of Hummel's Weimar Years
Illustrating the Importance of England and France

The following list of Hummel's compositions of the Weimar years, which clearly shows the significance of England and France for his work, has been compiled from dated manuscripts, references in letters, *etc.*, newspaper advertisements, and publication information. (For a complete list of Hummel's music, see this author's checklist in *Notes,* XXX/4 [June, 1974], 732-53. "S" numbers correspond to that list.) Works from earlier years that were published after 1819 are not included; compositions that are actually revisions of earlier works have been included but enclosed in parentheses. Italicized dates are taken from autographs and presumably indicate the time of completion. Other dates are, of course, somewhat approximate. Music known to have been composed for Weimar occasions is indicated by **W**; that composed on commission from or for tours to England or France is marked **E**, **F**, or **E-F**; arrangements, which absorbed a great deal of Hummel's energy, are included here. Regarding J.R. Schultz, who solicited many compositions and arrangements, see above, page 39, footnote 11. Arrangements are grouped at the end of each year's listings.

1819

E Trio, piano, violin and cello (Op. 83). For J.R. Schultz.
(Before September.)

Concerto, piano and orchestra (Op. 89). *October 1819.*

E Overture by Himmel, arr. piano, violin, and cello (S. 106a).
For J.R. Schultz? *1819.*

E Overture by Himmel (the same), arr. piano four-hands (S. 106b).
For J.R. Schultz? *1819.*

1820

W March inserted in Weigl's *Hadrian* (S. 106c). For a performance
September 16.

Potpourri, viola and orchestra (Op. 94) or cello and orchestra
(Op. 95). *September 1820.*

Waltzes for the Apollo-Saal [Vienna] 1821, for orchestra (published in piano reduction as Op. 91). *November 1820.*

Sonata, piano four-hands (Op. 92). For Anton Diabelli. *November 1820.*

E Overture, "Prometheus" (Beethoven), arr. piano, flute, violin, and cello (S. 107). For J.R. Schultz.

Variations, piano and orchestra (Op. 97). (Revision of earlier work?)

Variation on a theme of Anton Diabelli (S. 161). *ca.* 1820.

1821

(Trio, piano, violin and cello [Op. 93]. Revision of a work from the 1790's. *June 1821*).

(Trio, piano, violin and cello [Op. 96]. Completed about the same time as Op. 93 and probably a revision of an earlier work.)

W (Opera, *Mathilde von Guise*, [Op. 100]. Revised version for performance March 3; original composition: 1809-10.)

Piano Method (S. 157) was begun about this time, completed 1825.

E Arrangements of various Overtures, for piano, flute, violin, and cello (S. 108-130). Altogether Hummel arranged 24, of which the "Prometheus" arrangement (see 1820) was the first. No scores are dated; only "Prometheus," as the first of the series, was registered for copyright and therefore can be dated. The other Overture— arrangements were probably completed at a rate of three or four per year. All were written for J.R. Schultz or T. Boosey.

1822

W Festival Song, "Heute lasst" (text: Riemer; S. 158). For Goethe's birthday, August 28.

Nocturne, piano four-hands and two horns (Op. 99). *1822.*

(Variations, oboe and orchestra, Op. 102—an arrangement of Op. 99.)

Piano Method (see 1821).

E Arrangements of Overtures (see 1821).

1823

W Rondo, piano and orchestra (Op. 98). Before February 2.

W Cantata for the birthday of the Hereditary Grand Duke (S. 159), for February 2. Slightly revised (S. 160) for May 18.

E 3 Waltz-Rondos, piano (Op. 103). For J.R. Schultz. Before May 3.

F Accompaniments for two Romances (voice and piano), by Pierre Hédouin (S. 151). Possibly fraudulent.

Piano Method (see 1821).

E Arrangements for piano, flute, violin, and cello of Mozart, Symphonies K. 504, 550, 551 (S. 151, 152, 156). For J.R. Schultz. Early 1823 at the latest.

E Arrangements of Overtures (see 1821).

1824

E Sonata, cello and piano (Op. 104). For J.R. Schultz. Before January 31.

Sonata, piano (Op. 106). For Anton Diabelli. *March 1824.*

Bagatelles, piano (Op. 107). For C.F. Peters. Completed by April 23.

3 Amusements, piano (Op. 105). For C.F. Peters. Before May 3.

E (3 pieces, piano, for *The Harmonicon*, revised from ballets of *ca.* 1800-1810. [Also published in pirated editions as 3 Pièces faciles, Op. 111; S. 162, 164, 165.] For J.R. Schultz.)

Piano Method (see 1821).

E Arrangements of Mozart Symphonies K. 543, 425, 385, for piano, flute, violin, and cello (S. 153-155). For J.R. Schultz. Possibly as early as 1823.

E Arrangement of Beethoven Symphony No. 1, for piano, flute, violin, and cello (S. 137). For J.R. Schultz. By November 24.

E Arrangements of Overtures (see 1821).

1825

W Song, "Einmal nur," tenor and chorus (S. 166).

F Amusement, piano and violin (Op. 108). For the Duchess of Berry. *May 1825.*

Album piece (canon) for F. Hiller (S. 167a). *June 17.*

Rondo, piano (Op. 109). *September 1825.*

Piano Method completed, autumn.

W Music for the Jubilee of Grand Duke Karl August, *Morgenopfer* (Cantata, text by Goethe; song, text by St. Schütze; Serenade for orchestra; S. 170). For September 3-6.

W Part-song, "Herauf Gesang," for Goethe's 50th anniversary at Weimar (S. 167). By November 7.

Album-piece for Tobias Haslinger (lost; not verifiable. Probably autumn.)

F Album-piece for Maurice Schlesinger (lost; not verifiable). Late autumn.

E Arrangement of Beethoven Symphony No. 5, for piano, flute, violin, and cello (S. 135). For J.R. Schultz. By November 2.

E Arrangements of Overtures (see 1821).

F Opera, Attila (text: Jouy; S. 163). Incomplete; lost.

1826

W Song, "Strahlen die aus Osten stammen" (text: Peucer; S. 171), for Masonic Lodge Festival, September 15.

E (Scotland) 5 Settings of Scottish songs for George Thomson[1] (S. 169a-e).

F Attila (see 1825).

E Arrangements of Overtures (see 1821).

1827

W (Cantata for February 2 [S. 172] revision of S. 73 and S. 77 from 1806, 1807.)

Album piece for Franz Kandler, Vienna, April 8 (lost; not verifiable).

W Song, "Kehrt der frohe Tag" (S. 173), for Goethe's birthday, August 28.

Concerto, piano and orchestra, A flat (Op. 113). Autumn-winter.

E Arrangement of Beethoven, Septet, for piano, flute, violin, and cello (S. 150), *Finis January 1827.*

E Arrangement of A. Romberg, Symphony No. 1, for piano, flute, violin, and cello (S. 174). *October 1827.*

E Arrangement of Mozart, Piano Concerto K. 466, for piano, flute, violin, and cello (S. 138).

E Arrangements of Overtures (see 1821).

1828

(Album piece for Frau von Nass [excerpt from Septet Op. 74].)

Chorus, "Have' (S. 175).

W *Trauermusik*, chorus and four horns (S. 178), for the funeral of Grand Duke Carl August, June 14.

E Arrangement of Mozart, Piano Concerto K. 503, for piano, flute, violin, and cello (S. 139). Probably in the summer.

E Arrangement of Beethoven, Symphony No. 6, for piano, flute, violin, and cello (S. 136).

E Arrangements of Overtures (see 1821).

---

[1] For further details see Joel Sachs, "Hummel and George Thomson of Edinburgh," *op. cit.*

1829

W Cantata (S. 179), for the engagement of Prince Wilhelm of Prussia and Princess Augusta of Saxe-Weimar, February 16.

W Song, "Wir steigen" (text: St. Schütze; S. 180), for Goethe's birthday, August 28.

E-F? "Gesellschafts-Rondo" for piano and orchestra (Op. 117). *September 1829.*

E-F Septet (Op. 114). *October.*

E-F Fantasy, piano and orchestra, "Oberons Zauberhorn" (Op. 116). *November.*

W? "Volkslied aller Deutschen," for soloists, chorus, orchestra (S. 176).

E (Scotland) 12 Settings of folk songs for George Thomson (S. 178a-1).

E Arrangement of Mozart, 2-Piano Concerto K. 316a, for piano, flute, violin, and cello (S. 140). *August 1829.*

E Arrangement of Beethoven, Symphony No. 4, for piano, flute, violin, and cello (S. 134). Probably 1829.

E Arrangements of Overtures (see 1821).

1830

E-F? Variations, piano and orchestra, on a theme from *Das Fest der Handwerker* (Op. 115). *January 1830.*

E Variations for voice and orchestra, Op. 118, for Mme. Malibran. *ca.* 1829-30.

E Canon for Vincent Novello's album (S. 189). *July 1.*

E Piano piece for *Apollo's Gift, 1831* (S. 188). *July 1.*

E Variation on "Rule Britannia" (composite work with Cramer, Kalkbrenner Moscheles; S. 187). Spring or early summer.

E Canon, "Think on your friend" (S. 186). During the English tour or 1830, or possibly the tours of 1831 or 1833.

E Piano piece, F major (Op. post. 9f). Written at the same time as the above canon.

E Rondo, piano and orchestra. "Le Retour à (de) Londres" (Op. 127). Autumn.

E Arrangement of Mozart, Piano Concerto K. 456, for piano, flute, violin, and cello (S. 144). *January 1830.*

E Arrangement of Mozart, Piano Concerto K. 491, for piano, flute, violin, and cello (S. 141). *Fine 1830.*

E Arrangements of Overtures (see 1821).

1831

W 2 Part-Songs for Mme. Mara's birthday (S. 193). Completed by February 1.

E 3 sets of variations, piano (Op. 119; also published as Op. 120). Spring 1831.

E Rondo, piano, "La Galante" (Op. 120; also published as Op. 121). Spring 1831.

E Rondo "Villageois," piano (Op. 122). Probably spring, 1831.

E Fantasy, piano, "Recollections of Paganini" (S. 190). Spring?

E Romance, voice (and piano?), "Doubt not love" (S. 192). Spring, 1831? (lost; not verifiable).

E Impromptu, piano (S. 194), for Miss Harvey. *July 16.*

W Song, "Lieblich war der Traum" (text:?; S. 195). For Goethe's birthday, August 28.

F Etude, piano, B-flat (S. 191) for Fétis, *Méthode des Méthodes.*

E Arrangement of Haydn, Symphony No. 102, for piano, flute, violin, and cello (S. 182). *November 1831.*

E Arrangement of Haydn, Symphony No. 100, for piano, flute, violin, and cello (S. 183). *December 1831.*

E Arrangements of Overtures (see 1821).

1832

W Epilogue for Gluck, *Armide* (S. 198). For a performance February 16.

E (Scotland) Settings of 3 Scottish folksongs for George Thomson (S. 197).

W Part-Song, "Lasst fahren hin" (text: Goethe; S. 196) for memorial ceremony for Goethe, November 9.

E Arrangement of Beethoven, Symphony No. 3, for piano, flute, violin, and cello (S. 133). Early 1832 or possibly late 1831.

E Arrangement of Haydn, Symphony No. 103, for piano, flute, violin, and cello (S. 184). *February 1832.*

E Arrangement of Haydn, Symphony No. 44, for piano, flute, violin, and cello (S. 185). *June 1832.*

1833

E Concerto, piano and orchestra, F-major (Op. post. No. 1). *February 1833.*

E Finale to Act III of Hérold's *Zampa* (S. 200). By March 1833. (Lost)

E? Fantasies for piano, Opp. 123 and 124. Spring, 1833?

E Cantata, "The Orphan's Ode to the Patriots" (text: "The Lady of Dunstaffnage" [Anna Harrah McColl]; S. 199). Spring, 1833.

F? Etudes, piano, Op. 125. Before summer.

F Six new Etudes for Op. 125. August 1833.

1834

W Ballet music for *Der Löwe von Kurdistan* (Auffenberg). Partially a new version of excerpts from *Sappho*, Op. 68; otherwise S. 201). For February 8.

Rondo, violin or flute and piano (Op. 126). *September.*

W? Canon, "Muntre Gärten" (S. 202). *ca.* January.

1835

W Part-Song, "Landestreu" (S. 203), for the Liedertafel.

E Arrangement of Mozart, Piano Concerto K. 537, for piano, flute, violin, and cello (S. 142). *March 1835.*

E Arrangement of Beethoven, Symphony No. 7, for piano, flute, violin, and cello (S. 137). *May 1835.*

1836

W Finale for Act V of Auber's *Gustave III* (S. 204). For February 16.

W Impromptu for 2 pianos (S. 205), for Max Seidel. *December 24.*

E Arrangement of Mozart, Piano Concerto K. 482, for piano, flute, violin, and cello (S. 143). *January 1836.*

1837

W Ballet to conclude Hérold's *La Clochette* (S. 206). For February 2.

Supplement

The following works probably stem from the Weimar period but could not be dated.

(Overture, D-major, orchestra [revision of Op. 61; S. 148]. 1820's) Introduction and variations on a German song, flute or violin, and piano, Op. post. No. 2.

E? Scotch Country-Dance-Rondo, for piano, Op. post. No. 2. (1830's?).

Quartet, piano, violin, viola, cello (incomplete). Op. post. No. 4.

2 Capriccois, 2 Impromptus, Rondo, piano. Op. post. 9a-e.

Romance (untexted), voice and piano (S. 144).

E Arrangement of Beethoven, Symphony No. 2, for piano, flute, violin, and cello (S. 132).

Cantata, "Heil diesem Tag" (unverifiable).

Bibliography

The following bibliography does not include biographical articles from standard reference works such as *Grove's Dictionary*, *Die Musik in Geschichte und Gegenwart*, *Biographie Universelle* (Fétis), *Dictionary of National Biography*, and *Biographie Universelle* (Michaud).

General Newspapers

Le Courrier (later: *Le Courrier Français*). Paris.

La Gazette de France. Paris.

La Gazette de Paris. Paris.

John Bull. London.

Journal des Débats Politiques et Littéraires. Paris.

The Morning Chronicle. London.

The Norwich Mercury. Norwich.

The Times. London.

Music Periodicals

Allgemeine musikalische Zeitung. Edited by J.F. Rochlitz *et alii*. Leipzig: Breitkopf und Härtel, 1798-1848.

Allgemeine musikalische Zeitung mit besonderer Rücksicht auf den Österreichischen Kaiserstaat. Edited by I.F. von Mosel *et alii*. Vienna: S.A. Steiner, 1817-1824.

Allgemeiner musikalischer Anzeiger. Edited by I.F. Castelli. Vienna: Haslinger, 1829-1840.

Berliner Allgemeine musikalische Zeitung. Edited by A.B. Marx. Berlin: Schlesinger, 1824-1830.

Cäcilia: eine Zeitschrift für die musikalische Welt. Edited by G. Weber. Mainz: B. Schott, 1824-1848.

The English Musical Gazette; or, Monthly Intelligencer. Edited by T. Busby. London: Arding and Merrett, 1819.

The Flutist's Magazine. Edited by W.N. James. London: Boosey, 1827.

The Flutonicon; or Flute Player's Monthly Magazine. London, 1834-1846.

La France Musicale. Edited by M. and L. Escudier. Paris: 1837-1870.

Gazette Musicale de Paris. Edited by M. Schlesinger. Paris: Lachevardière, 1834-1835.

The Giulianiad, or Guitarist's Magazine. London: Sherwood, 1833-1834.

The Harmonicon. Edited by W. Ayrton. London: Pinnock, 1823-1833.

Iris im Gebiete der Tonkunst. Edited by L. Rellstab. Berlin: Trautwein, 1830-1841.

Le Ménestrel, Journal de Musique. Edited by J. Heugel *et alii*. Paris, 1833-1940.

The Monthly Magazine of Music. London: Whittaker, 1823.

The Monthly Musical and Literary Magazine. London: James Fraser, 1830.

The Monthly Musical Journal, Consisting of Original British and of New Foreign Music, Vocal and Instrumental. "Conducted by Dr. [Thomas] Busby." London: Phillips, 1800.

The Musical Journal, A Magazine of Information on All Subjects Connected with the Science. London: Limbird, 1840.

The Musical Library. Edited by W. Ayrton. London: Knight, 1834-1837.

The Musical Magazine. London: F. De Porquet and Cooper, 1835.

The Musical World, A Weekly Record of Musical Science, Literature, and Intelligence. Edited by C. Clarke *et alii*. London: Novello, 1836-1891.

Musikalische Eilpost. Übersicht des Neuesten im Gebiete der Musik. Edited by J.G. Häser and J.C. Lobe. Weimar: Wilhelm Hoffmann, 1826.

Neue Zeitschrift für Musik. Edited by R. Schumann *et alii*. Leipzig: Barth, *etc*., 1834-.

The New Musical Magazine, Review, and Register of Valuable Musical Publications, Ancient and Modern. London: C. Cook, *etc*., 1809.

The Philharmonicon, A Periodical of Piano-Forte and Vocal Music. London: Sherwood, *ca*. 1833.

Le Pianiste. Edited by J. Delacour. Paris: 1833-1834.

The Quarterly Musical Magazine and Review. Edited by R.M. Bacon. London, 1818-*ca*. 1828.

Revue et Gazette Musicale de Paris. Edited by M. Schlesinger *et alii*. Paris: Schlesinger, 1835-1880.

La Revue Musicale. "Publiée par [F.J.] Fétis. Paris, 1827-1835.

Wiener Pfennig-Magazin für das Piano-Forte. Edited by C. Czerny. Vienna: Haslinger, 1835.

Other Periodicals

The Athenaeum. London Literary and Critical Journal. Edited by J.S. Buckingham. London.

Le Corsaire. Journal de Littérature. "Par X.Y.Z." Poitiers, Paris.

Courrier des Théâtres, Littérature, Beaux-Arts, Sciences, Histoire, Industrie, Moeurs, Librairie, Variétés, Nouvelles, Modes. Edited by C. Maurice. Paris.

The Court Journal. London.

Le Globe, Journal littéraire. Paris.

The Ladies Cabinet of Fashion, Music & Romance. Edited by M. and B. de Courcy. London.

Mechanic's Magazine. Edited by I.C. Robertson *et alii.* London.

The Penny Mechanic. A Magazine of the Arts and Sciences. London.

Der Sammler: Ein Unterhaltungsblatt. Edited by I. von Portenschlag *et alii.* Vienna.

The Spectator. London.

Wiener Theater-Zeitung. (later: *Wiener allgemeine Theaterzeitung.*) Edited by C. Bolthart *et alii.* Vienna, Trieste.

Wiener Zeitschrift für Kunst, Literatur, Theater und Mode. Edited by J. Schickh. Vienna.

Musical Annuals and Other Collections of Music

Apollo's Gift, or the Musical Souvenir for 1830 (1831). Edited by M. Clementi and J.B. Cramer. London: Chappell, *etc.*, 1829-1830.

The Beauties of Mozart, Handel, Pleyel, Haydn, Beethoven, and other Celebrated Composers, adapted to the Words of Popular Psalms & Hymns for One or Two Voices, Piano Forte, Organ or Harp, By an Eminent Professor. London: Leigh, *ca.* 1820.

The Cadeau: A Christmas, New-Year's, Midsummer, or Birth-Day Present for 1831 (1832). London: Johanning and Whatmore, 1830-1831.

The Harmonist, A select Collection of Ancient & Modern Glees, Catches, Canons, Epigrams &c. 15 vols. London: Wheatstone, *ca.* 1817-*ca.* 1825.

La Lyre d'Apollon, A Collection of Marches & Polonoises for the Piano Forte by the best Foreign Authors. London: Wessel & Stodart, *ca.* 1830.

The Minstrel's Offering, or Musical Anthology for 1831. Edited by N.C. Bochsa and W.T. Moncrieff. London: Bochsa, 1830.

The Monthly Polite Musical Repertory. London: Longman, *ca.* 1805.

Musica Antiqua. Edited by J.S. Smith. 2 vols. London: Preston, 1812.

The Musical Album for 1834. London: H. Falkner, 1833.

The Musical Bijou, An Album of Music, Poetry, and Prose. Edited by F.H. Burney. London: Goulding and D'Almaine, 1829-1851.

The Musical Forget-Me-Not, A Cabinet of Music and Poetry, for 1832. Edited by T. Mackinlay. London: Ackermann, 1831.

The Musical Gem: A Souvenir for 1830 (-1832). Edited by W. Ball *et alii.* London: Mori and Lavenu, 1829-1831.

The Musical Guide. Edited by "W.H.P." London: G. Berger, 1834.

The Musical Keepsake for the Year 1834. London: Longman, Rees, Orme, Brown, and Green, 1833.

The Musical Talisman for 1835. London: D'Almaine, 1834.

The Nosegay, A Cage d'Amour & Musical Cadeau. Edited by F.W.N. Bayley and J.F. Danneley. London: Danneley, 1832.

Sacred Minstrelsy: A Collection of Sacred Music by the Great Masters of All Ages and Nations; Consisting of Anthems, Solos, Duets, Trios, &c., and Choruses; with Accompaniments for the Piano-Forte or Organ. Edited by W. Ayrton. 2 vols. London: John William Parker, 1834-1835.

La Salle d'Apollon, A Collection of New and Elegant German Waltzes for the Piano Forte, Composed by the most esteemed Foreign Authors. London: Wessel & Stodart, 1825-1830.

Selection of Sacred Music from the Works of Some of The Most Eminent Composers of Germany and Italy. Edited by C.I. Latrobe. London: Birchall, Lonsdale, 1806-*ca.* 1826.

Books and Articles

Academy of Vocal Harmony. Pamphlet. London, 1840.

Bartels, Adolf. *Chronik des Weimarischen Hoftheaters 1817-1907. Festschrift zur Einweihung des neuen Hoftheater-Gebäudes, 11. Januar 1908.* Weimar: Hermann Böhlaus, 1908.

Batka, Johann, and Wodiáner, Emerich. *Johann Nepomuk Hummel: Biographische Skizze. Zur Enthüllung des Hummel-Denkmals.* Pressburg: Denkmal-Comité, 1887.

[Beethoven, Ludwig van.] *The Letters of Beethoven.* Collected and translated by Emily Anderson. 3 vols. London: Macmillan, 1961.

Benyovsky, Karl. *J.N. Hummel: Der Mensch und Künstler.* Bratislava-Pressburg: Eos, 1934.

————. *Joh. Nep. Hummel und Eisenstadt.* ("Burgenländischen Heimatblatter," Jahrgang 6.) Eisenstadt, 1937.

————. *Hummel und seine Vaterstadt.* Bratislava-Pressburg: Steiner, 1937.

[Boosey, Thomas.] *New and Classical Music, by the most Admired Foreign Composers, just published by T. Boosey and Co.* London: Boosey, 1818.

————. *Selection of Admired Compositions contained in T. Boosey & Co.'s General Catalogue of Foreign Music & Supplement.* London: Boosey, ca. 1820.

Boyle's New Fashionable Court and Country Guide and Town Visiting Directory. London: George Boyle, 1796-1924.

Brayley, Edward Wedlake. *Historical and Descriptive Accounts of the Theatres of London.* London: J. Taylor, 1826.

Brémont, Anna, Comtesse de. *The World of Music: The Great Virtuosi.* London: Gibbings, 1892.

Brock, David G.: "The Church Music of Hummel." *Music Review*, XXXI (1970), 249-54.

[Chopin, Frédéric.] *Correspondance de Frederic Chopin.* Translated and edited by Bronislaw Sydow *et alii.* 3 vols. Paris: Richard - Masse, 1953-1960.

Clément, Félix, and Larousse, Pierre. *Dictionnaire des Opéras.* Paris: Larousse, 1905.

Courcy, Geraldine I.C. de. *Paganini the Genoese.* 2 vols. Norman: University of Oklahoma Press, 1957.

Crotch, William. *Substance of Several Courses of Lectures on Music, Read in the University of Oxford, and in the Metropolis.* London: Longman, Rees, Orme, Brown, and Green, 1831.

Czerny, Carl. "Recollections from my Life." Translated by Ernest Sanders. *The Musical Quarterly*, XLII (1956), 302-17.

Davis, Richard. "The Music of J.N. Hummel, its Derivations and Development." *Music Review*, XXVI (1965), 169-91.

Decourcelle, Maurice. *La Société Académique des Enfants d'Apollon (1741-1880).* Paris: Durand, Schoenewerk, 1881.

Deutsch, Otto Erich (collector and editor). *Schubert: Memoirs by his Friends.* Translated by Rosamond Ley and John Nowell. London: Black, 1958.

————. *The Schubert Reader: A Life of Franz Schubert in Letters and Documents.* Translated by Eric Blom. New York: Norton, 1947.

Dibdin, Charles Jr. *History and Illustrations of the London Theatres.* London: For the Proprietors of "Illustrations of London Buildings," 1826.

Doran, John. *Memoir of Queen Adelaide, Consort of King William IV.* London: Richard Bentley, 1861.

Elkin, Robert. *Royal Philharmonic: The Annals of the Royal Philharmonic Society.* London: Rider, 1947.

Fétis, François Joseph. *Biographie Universelle des Musiciens et Bibliographie Générale de la Musique.* 8 vols. 2d ed. Paris: Firmin Didot, 1867-1870.

Foster, Myles Birket. *History of the Philharmonic Society of London 1813-1912.* London: Lane, 1912.

Frimmel, Theodor (ed.). *Beethoven Forschung; lose Blätter.* 10 vols. Vienna: Gerold, 1911-1925.

Gardiner, William. *Music and Friends; or, Pleasant Recollections of A Dilettante.* 3 vols. London: Longman, Orme, Brown, and Longman, 1838-1853.

Genast, Eduard. *Aus dem Tagebuche eines alten Schauspielers.* 2 vols. Leipzig: Voigt und Günther, 1862.

Gotch, Rosamund Brunel (ed). *Mendelssohn and his Friends in Kensington: Letters from Fanny and Sophy Horsley written 1833-36.* London: Oxford University Press, 1934.

[Guichard, C.] *Catalogue of New Music Published and Sold by C. Guichard at Bossange and Masson, 14 Great Marlborough Street.* Pamphlet. London, 1816.

Hadden, J. Cuthbert. *George Thomson, The Friend of Burns: His Life and Correspondence.* London: Nimmo, 1898.

Hadow, Sir William Henry. *A Croatian Composer. Notes Toward the Study of Joseph Haydn.* London: Seeley, 1897.

Harich, Johann. *Esterházy-Musikgeschichte im Speigel der zeitgenössischen Textbücher.* Eisenstadt: Rötzer, 1959.

Highfill, Philip Jr. "Communication." *Journal of the American Musicological Society,* IX (1956), 70-71.

Hiller, Ferdinand. *Künstlerleben.* Cologne: Dumont-Schauberg, 1880.

Hirsch, Rudolf. *Gallerie Lebender Tondichter.* Güns: Reichard, 1836.

Hogarth, George. *Musical History, Biography, and Criticism: Being a General Survey of Music, from the Earliest Period to the Present Time.* London: Parker, 1835.

Kahlert, August. "Zur Erinnerung an Johann Nepomuk Hummel." *Deutsche Musik-Zeitung,* February 11, 1860, pp. 50-51; February 18, 1860, pp. 58-59; February 25, 1860, pp. 67-68.

La Mara [Marie Lipsius]. *Musikerbriefe aus fünf Jahrhunderten.* 2 vols. Leipzig: Breitkopf und Härtel, 1886.

Landon, H.C. Robbins. *The Collected Correspondence and London Notebooks of Joseph Haydn.* London: Barrie and Rockliff, 1959.

[Liszt, Franz]. *Briefwechsel zwischen Franz Liszt und Carl Alexander, Grossherzog von Sachsen.* Edited by La Mara [Marie Lipsius]. Leipzig: Brietkopf und Härtel, 1909.

————. *Correspondance de Liszt et de la Comtesse d'Agoult, 1833-1840.* Publiée par Daniel Ollivier. Paris: Grasset, 1933.

————. *Franz Liszt's Briefe.* Collected and edited by La Mara [Marie Lipsius]. 8 vols. Leipzig: Breitkopf und Härtel, 1893-1905.

Loewe, Carl. *Carl Loewe's Selbstbiographie.* Edited by C.H. Bitter. Berlin: Wilhelm Müller, 1870.

Loewenberg, Alfred (comp.). *Annals of Opera, 1597-1940.* 2 vols. 2d ed. Geneva: Societas Bibliographica, 1955.

London Academy of Music. Pamphlet, London, *ca.* 1840.

Mackerness, Eric David. *A Social History of English Music.* London: Routledge and Kegan Paul, 1964.

[Mendelssohn-Bartholdy, Felix]. *Briefe einer Reise durch Deutschland, Italien und die Schweiz.* Edited by Peter Sutermeister. Zürich: Niehans, 1958.

—————. *Felix Mendelssohn-Bartholdys Briefwechsel mit Legationsrat Karl Klingemann in London.* Edited by Karl Klingemann. Essen: Baedeker, 1909.

—————. *Letters.* Edited by Gisella Selden-Goth. New York: Pantheon, 1945.

Milde, Theodor. *Über das Leben und die Werke der beliebtesten deutschen Tonsetzer.* Meissen: Goedsche, 1834.

Mitchell, Francis Humphries. "The Piano Concertos of Johann Nepomuk Hummel." Dissertation, Northwestern University, 1957.

Morris, Lydia T. *Famous Musical Composers. Being Biographies of Eminent Musicians.* 2d ed. London: Unwin, 1892.

Moscheles, Charlotte (ed.). *Aus Moscheles' Leben.* 2 vols. Leipzig: Duncker und Humblot, 1872-1873.

Münster, Robert. "Authentische Tempi zu den sechs letzten Sinfonien W.A. Mozarts?" *Mozart Jahrbuch 1962/63,* (Salzburg: Internationale Stiftung Mozarteum, 1964), pp. 185-99.

Neumann, W[illiam?]. *Die Componisten der neueren Zeit.* Cassel: Balde, 1857.

[Novello and Co.]. *A Century and a Half in Soho: A Short History of the Firm of Novello, Publishers and Printers of Music, 1811-1961.* London: Novello, 1961.

Pohl, Karl Ferdinand. *Mozart und Haydn in London.* 2 vols. Vienna: Carl Gerold's Sohn, 1867.

Raabe, Peter. *Franz Liszt.* 2 vols. Stuttgart: Cotta, 1931.

Raymond-Duval, P.H. "Le Romantisme: 1815 à 1837." *Encyclopédie de la Musique et Dictionnaire du Conservatoire,* (11 vols.; Paris: Delagrave, 1921-1931), II, 1061 ff.

Riemann, Hugo. *Opern Handbuch.* Leipzig: Seemann, 1886.

Sachs, Joel. "A Checklist of the Works of Johann Nepomuk Hummel." *Notes,* XXX (1974), 732-54.

—————. "Authentic English and French Editions of J.N. Hummel." *Journal of the American Musicological Society,* XXV (1972), 203-29.

—————. "Hummel and George Thomson of Edinburgh." *Musical Quarterly,* LVI (1970), 270-87.

—————. "Hummel and the Pirates: The Struggle for Musical Copyright." *Musical Quarterly,* LIX (1973), 31-60.

————. "Hummel in England and France: A Study in the International Musical Life of the Early Nineteenth Century." Dissertation, Columbia University, 1968.

Schemann, Ludwig. *Cherubini.* Stuttgart: Deutsche Verlags-Anstalt, 1925.

Schlesinger, Thea. *Johann Baptist Cramer und seine Klaviersonaten.* Munich: Knorr und Hirth, 1928.

Schmieder, Wolfgang. "Hummel-Dokumente eines alten Musikverlagsarchiv." *Allgemeine Musikzeitung,* LXIV (1937), 608-9.

[Schumann, Robert]. *Gesammelte Schriften über Musik und Musiker.* Edited by Martin Kreisig. 5th ed. 2 vols. Leipzig: Brietkopf und Härtel, 1914.

————. *Jugendbriefe von Robert Schumann.* Edited by Clara Schumann. Leipzig: Brietkopf und Härtel, 1885.

————. *Der Junge Schumann: Dichtungen und Briefe.* Edited by Alfred Schumann. Leipzig: Insel, 1910.

————. *Robert Schumann's Briefe. Neue Folge.* Edited by F. Gustav Jansen. Zweite vermehrte und verbesserte Auflage. Leipzig: Brietkopf und Härtel, 1904.

Seidel, Max Johann. "Biographische Notizen aus dem Leben des am 17ten. October 1837 verstorbenen Grossherzoglich-Sachsen-Weimarischen Kapellmeister und Ritter mehreren Orden Johann Nepomuk Hummel, ersten Klavierspieler seiner Zeit." Manuscript, Weimar, *ca.* 1837.

Sietz, Reinhold. *Aus Ferdinand Hillers Briefwechsel. (Beiträge zur rheinischen Musikgeschichte, Hefte 28, 48, 56, 60, 65, 70.)* 6 vols. Cologne: Arno, 1958-1968.

[Spohr, Louis]. *The Musical Journeys of Ludwig Spohr.* Translated and edited by Henry Pleasants. Norman: University of Oklahoma Press, 1961.

————. *Selbstbiographie.* 2 vols. Reprint. Kassel: Barenreiter, 1954.

Thayer, Alexander Wheelock. *Thayer's Life of Beethoven.* Revised and edited by Elliot Forbes. 2 vols. Princeton: Princeton University Press, 1967.

Towers, John (comp.). *Dictionary-Catalogue of Operas and Operettas Which Have Been Performed on the Public Stage.* Morgantown: Acme, 1910.

Tyson, Alan. *The Authentic English Editions of Beethoven.* London: Faber and Faber, 1963.

————. "J.R. Schultz and his visit to Beethoven," *Musical Times,* LXII (1972), 450-51.

Unger, Max. *Muzio Clementis Leben.* Printed dissertation, Leipzig, 1913.

[Weber, Carl Maria von]. *Reise-Briefe von Carl Maria von Weber an seine Gattin Carolina.* Edited by Carl von Weber. Leipzig: Dürr, 1886.

Werner, Eric. Mendelssohn: *A New Image of the Composer and his Age.* Translated by Dika Newlin. New York: Free Press of Glencoe, 1963.

Zimmerschied, Dieter. "Die Kammermusik Johann Nepomuk Hummels." Dissertation, Mainz, 1966.

Zimmerschied, Dieter. *Thematisches Verzeichnis der Werke von Johann Nepomuk Hummel*. Hofheim: Hofmeister, 1971. Users should consult review by Joel Sachs, *Musical Times*, CXIV (1973), 898-99.

Biographical Glossary and Index

Since many of the figures in this book were extremely famous in their day and are now virtually forgotten, I have identified each person briefly. In some cases, the miniscule information is in fact all that I have been able to unearth about them, even though their names occur quite frequently in concert life. In most cases, however, I have at least been able to provide their first names, an attribute almost always lacking in programs and in reviews. For those who have already been identified in the text of this book, I have provided a boldface reference to the point of identification, in order to conserve space by avoiding mere repetition. Sources of information include nineteenth- and twentieth-century biographical dictionaries, records of the Philharmonic Society and Royal Society of Musicians, Philharmonic, Antient Concert, and other concert programs, letters, and the occasional reference in a newspaper report. A few people have nevertheless defied identification.

ADAM, Adolphe (1803-1856). French opera and ballet composer.
Faust, 82n8, 85

ADELAIDE of Saxe-Meiningen (1792-1849). Duchess of Clarence and Queen of England (1830-1837).
45, 63, 64, 67, 68, 73, 74, 74n20, 76, 76n23, 81, 83, 88, 89

ALSAGER, Thomas Massa (1779-1846). Proprietor of *The Times*; his suggestion is said to have led to the first employment of a music critic by a daily newspaper. He was a fine amateur musician, capable of playing all the orchestral instruments. Alsager's private concerts, the Queen Square Select Society, London, evolved into the Beethoven Quartet Society.
43, 43n22

ANDERSON, George Frederick (1793-1876). Violinist in the leading London orchestras, member of the Philharmonic Society and its treasurer from 1840 until his death. Master of the Queen's Musick, 1848-1870.
41n17, 61, 69

ANDERSON, Lucy Philpot

41, **41n17**, 42, 43, 52, 54, 58, 61, 62, 63, 66, 67n3, 71, 74, 86

ASPULL, George

42, **42n19**, 87n18

ASPULL, William (?-   ?). Brother of George Aspull, and organist of
St. Mary's Church, Nottingham, 1830-1835.

87, 87n18

ATTWOOD, Thomas (1765-1858). Organist of St. Paul's Cathedral, composer
of music for church and stage; one of the original members of the
Philharmonic Society and one of the first teachers at the Royal Academy
of Music. A student of Mozart.

74

AUBER, Daniel François Esprit (1782-1871). French opera composer.

47, 55, 57n48, 75 / *Gustave III*, 105

AUFFENBERG, Joseph Freiherr von (1798-1850). German playwright.

Der Löwe von Kurdistan, 105

AUGUSTA, Princess of England (1768-1840). Sixth child of King George III.

52

AUGUSTA, Princess of Saxe-Weimar (1811-1890). Later Queen and Empress of
Germany (wife of Wilhelm I); student of Hummel at Weimar.

103

AYRTON, William (1777-1858). Writer on music, founder of *The Harmonicon*;
critic for the *Morning Chronicle* and the *Examiner*. As musical director
of the King's Theatre he introduced *Don Giovanni*, *Così fan Tutte*, and
Die Zauberflöte to England. Member of the Philharmonic Society,
1813-1858.

37, 60, 89, 89n21, 90n22, 92

BACH, J.S. (1685-1750)

37 / *Fantasia and Fuge*, 91

BACON, Mary Anne (1800-1885)

62, **62n58**, 74n20

BACON, Richard Mackenzie (1776-1844). English author, music critic, and
businessman resident in Norwich. Bacon was founder, editor, and chief

writer for England's first important music journal, the *Quarterly Musical Magazine and Review* (1818-1828); he also wrote numerous political pamphlets. Father of Mary Anne Bacon.

62

BAILLOT, Pierre-Marie-François (1771-1842). One of France's greatest violinists. Director of the *Concerts Spirituels*, 1822-1824; first violin of the Royal Chapel, 1825ff.

22, 23, 32, 53 / *Variations for violin*, 24

BARNARD, Sir Andrew Francis

74, **74n20**

BARTON, Sir John (1771-1834). Secretary and treasurer to William IV when he was Duke of Clarence, and to Adelaide after their accession in 1830.

76n23

BEALE, John (*ca.* 1796-   ?). Pianist, pupil of J.B. Cramer. Associate of the Philharmonic Society, 1813-1819; member, 1820-1833. Professor at the Royal Academy of Music from its founding.

40

BEETHOVEN, Ludwig van (1770-1827)

9, 10, 36, 37, 39n11, 40, 42, 44, 60n55, 96, 96n10 / *Fidelio*, 79, 84, 85, 86n15 / *Overture, Prometheus*, 100 / *Septet*, 102 / *Symphonies: No. 1*, 101 / *No. 2*, 105 / *No. 3*, 104 / *No. 4*, 103 / *No. 5*, 101 / *No. 6*, 102 / *No. 7*, 105 / *No. 9*, 53 / *Trio Op. 3*, 60n55

BEGNIS, Giuseppe de (1793-1849). Italian bass singer. Paris debut, 1819; London debut, 1822 in *Il Turco in Italia*.

63

BELLEVILLE, Mlle. See Oury, Anna

BELLINI, Vincenzo (1801-1835). Italian opera composer.

86n17, 89n21

BENNETT, James (?-   ?). English tenor. He made numerous appearances at the Philharmonic Society in the 1830's and at the Concert of Antient Music through the 1840's, when he was also on the faculty of the Royal Academy of Music. Possibly the James Bennett (1804-1870) who wrote a didactic work.

67

BÉRIOT, Charles-Auguste de (1802-1870). Belgian violinist, student of Baillot; first chamber violinist to the King of France. He toured with Mme. Malibran

BORDOGNI (Bordagni), Marc(o) (1788-1856). Italian-born singer and professor of voice, engaged by the Théâtre Italien in Paris, 1819-1833; professor at the Paris Conservatory, 1820 ff.

22

BOUCHER, Alexandre-Jean (1770-1861). Parisian violinist and teacher of violin.

25n31

BOUCHER, Céleste Gallyot (?-1841). French harpist, active at least as early as 1794; wife of the above.

24, 25n31

BOWCHER. Chester music-dealer.

39

BRAHAM, John (1777-1856). Distinguished English tenor. Debut, Covent Garden, 1787. He sang Max in the English version of *Der Freischütz*, 1824, and Huon in the premiere of *Oberon*, 1826, under Weber. Associate of the Philharmonic, 1813-1844; member, 1815-1841.

91n24

BRIDGEMAN, Mrs. (?- ?). Unidentified pianist in Norwich.

72

BROD, Henri (1799-1839). Parisian oboist and composer; principal oboist at the Opéra and Société des Concerts du Conservatoire. Labored to improve the construction of the instrument.

22

BROSSIN. Unidentified opera singer.

82n7

BULL, Ole (1810-1880). Norwegian violin virtuoso and composer. After 1832 he enjoyed a sensational career, touring widely in Europe and North America, performing almost exclusively his own compositions and improvising.

91n24

BUSSE, (?). German (?) bass (?) singer, member of the Ottos' (*q.v.*) male singing group. Otherwise unidentified.

87

CAMUS, Paul-Hippolyte (1786- ?). Parisian composer and principal flutist of the Théâtre Italien.

Air varié, 33

CARL ALEXANDER (1818-1901). Grand-Duke of Saxe-Weimar (1853-1901).
92, 93

CARL AUGUST (1757-1828). Grand-Duke of Saxe-Weimar (1775-1828).
10, 18, 29, 30, 102

CARL FRIEDRICH (1783-1853). Grand-Duke of Saxe-Weimar (1828-1853).
30, 78

CAROLINE, Ferdinande Louise, Duchess of Berry (1798-1870). Daughter of
Francis I of Naples, wife of Prince Charles Ferdinand, Duke of Berry. In
addition to being a capable violinist, she was exiled and imprisoned for her
political activities.
23, 23n25, 35, 101

CASTELLI, Ignaz Friedrich (1781-1854). Viennese poet, writer for journals,
editor of the *Allgemeiner musikalischer Anzeiger* (Vienna, 1829-1840).
A close friend of the Hummels.
19, 77

CAWSE, Miss H. (?-   ?). English contralto; she sang at the Philharmonic
1830-1832.
73, 74

CHABROL de VOLVIC, Gilbert Joseph Gaspard, Count (1778-1842).
Counsellor of State, Prefect of the Département of the Seine and Oise,
therefore general administrator of Paris.
23n26

CHARLES X (1757-1836). King of France (1824-1830).
23, 27

CHELARD, Hippolyte-André-Jean-Baptiste (1789-1861). French composer,
active in Germany. Student of Zingarelli, Paisiello, and others. His most
famous opera: *Macbeth*. Chelard was successor to Hummel as Kapellmeister
in Weimar, and was himself succeeded by Liszt in 1848.
76, 79, 80, 81, 86n17 / *Metternacht,* 81

CHERUBINI, Luigi (1760-1842). Italo-French composer, director of the Paris
Conservatory.
18, 19, 19n11, 20, 24, 24n30, 25, 32, 64, 64n65 / *Les deux Journées,* 20 /
L'Hôtellerie portugaise, 24

CHILD, Miss E. (?-   ?). English pianist, student at the Royal Academy of Music, 1825-1830, and still living in London *ca.* 1848.
63

CHOPIN, Fryderyk Franciszek (1810-1849)
48

CHORON, Alexandre-Étienne (1771-1834). French writer on music, especially of didactic treatises; composer, publisher, founder of the government-supported Institution Royale de Musique Classique et Religieuse (1824-1830).
32

CIMAROSA, Domenico (1749-1841). Italian composer.
37

CINTI, Mlle. Early stage-name of Mme. Laure-Cinthie Montalant (1801-1863). Parisian soprano, known as an excellent singer with a very pure voice. After a career at the Opéra and the Théâtre Italien—an ardent supporter was Rossini—she taught voice at the Conservatory.
22, 24, 88

CINTI-DAMOREAU. See Cinti.

CLAUDE of Lorraine (1600-1682). French painter.
36

CLEMENTI, Muzio (1752-1832). Italian pianist, composer, publisher, instrument manufacturer, longtime resident of London.
19n12, 42, 44, 44n26

CLEMENTI & Co. London publishers and instrument makers.
39

COCKS, Robert and Co. London music sellers and publishers.
38, 39, 54, 73n14

CONYNGHAM, Henry (1766-1832). 1st Marquess Conyngham.
45n28

COOKE, Thomas Simpson (1782-1848). Distinguished singer and instrumentalist. In addition to being principal tenor at the Bavarian Embassy musical establishment and at Covent Garden Theatre, he played violin, flute, oboe, clarinet, bassoon, horn, cello, bass, and piano. He was a member of the Philharmonic, its leader for a number of years, and occasionally its conductor.

70, 90n22

CORELLI, Arcangelo (1653-1713). Italian composer.

37

CORNEGA, Mme. Nina (?-   ?). Italian soprano, a student of Salieri. She was a member of the San Carlo opera in Naples, and gave a very successful tour of Germany in 1823. Mme. Cornega was praised for pure intonation and dynamic range.

20

CRAMER, Miss (?-   ?). English singer, whose active career is marked by a singular lack of personal information. She was a child of Franz Cramer.

63, 73, 74

CRAMER, Franz (François, Francis) (1772-1848). Mannheim-born violinist, resident in London for most of his life, and younger brother of J.B. Cramer. He was one of the most active musicians in London: leader of most orchestras, professor at the Royal Academy of Music, many times a director of the Philharmonic Society. Although Cramer enjoyed a good reputation, Fétis felt that he was never more than a rather mediocre violinist. He was Master of the Queen's Musick from 1837 until his death.

70, 74, 89, 89n21

CRAMER, Johann (John) Baptist (1771-1858). Mannheim-born pianist, brought to London as an infant, where he studied with Clementi. He was one of England's favorite pianists in the early nineteenth century, and was also a renowned composer and successful publisher.

37, 42, 44, 44n24, 48, 54, 58, 66, 71, 74, 86n16, 91, 91n24, 92, 96, 103 / *Sonata Op. 63,* 44 / *Studies for piano,* 44

CZERNY, Carl (Karl) (1791-1857). Noted Viennese pianist, prolific composer, active teacher. He was a student of Beethoven and a good friend of Hummel.

27n33, 32, 42, 44n26

DANCE, William (1755-1840). One of the original proposers and founding members of the Philharmonic Society, and a director for twenty-two of the twenty-eight years in which he was a member. He was co-principal or principal violist of the orchestra until he retired in 1837, and treasurer, 1815, 1821-1822, and 1836-1838.

56n47, 57n49, 70, 89, 89n21

DAUPRAT, Louis-François (1781-1868). Parisian hornist and composer, a student of Gossec. He was solo hornist in the Opéra orchestra, professor at the Conservatoire, and a member of the chapel of Louisc XVIII.
22 / *Solo for French horn*, 21

DAVID, Ferdinand (1810-1873). German violinist and teacher, concertmaster of the Leipzig Gewandhaus orchestra under Mendelssohn, author of a very important treatise on violin playing. David was known for his part in the revival of eighteenth century masters.
53

DAVID, Louisa. See Dulcken.

DAVIES. Southampton music dealer.
39

DAVIS. Portsmouth music dealer.
39

DIABELLI, Anton (1781-1858). Viennese music dealer, publisher, and composer.
100, 101

DÖHLER, Theodor (1814-1856). Austrian pianist, born and resident in Italy. He was raised to the rank of nobility by the Duke of Lucca to permit his marriage to a Russian princess. Döhler ceased public performing *ca.* 1846.
91n24

DOLLE (Dölle) (?-   ?). Probably a German tenor at the Frankfurt opera who disappears into the shadow of his more famous wife in contemporary reports.
82n7

DONZELLI, Domenico (1790-1873). Italian tenor. His success began in Vienna, 1822, after which he was engaged in Paris (1824-1831) and London (1829 ff.).
24, 49, 82n8, 83, 87, 88

DORUS-GRAS, Mme. Julie-Aimée-Josèphe (1804-   ?). French soprano, student of Paer and Bordogni. She sang in *Le Comte Ory* at the Paris Opéra, 1830.
22, 23

DRAGONETTI, Domenico (1763-1846). Venetian double-bass player, resident in London from 1794 where he was the most sought-after bassist, commanding at times the highest wages of any player in the Philharmonic. He was the inseparable playing companion of cellist Robert Lindley, with whom he shared a stand for decades. Dragonetti also composed, and was involved in many businesses.

40, 42, 43, 44n25, 49, 59n51, 63, 69, 70n8, 72

DULCKEN, Lousia David

53, 53n44, 58, 71, 86

DUMONT, Louise. See Farrenc.

"DUNSTAFFNAGE, Lady of." See McColl.

DUSSEK, Jan Ladislav (1760-1812). Bohemian pianist and composer, a resident of London in the 1790's and early 1800's.

Concerto Op. 15, 51n39

ELIASON, Edward (?-   ?)

52

EHLERS, (?) (?-   ?)

82n7

ELSSLER, Franziska ("Fanny") (1810-1884). Noted Viennese ballet dancer, daughter of Haydn's copyist and servant Johann Elssler. She made her debut aged six or seven years, in a children's ballet at the Theater an der Wien. London debut, 1833. She retired in 1851.

82, 82n8, 85 / *Sonnambule divertissement*, 84

ELSSLER, Johann (1769-1843). Servant and copyist to Haydn.

82n8

ELSSLER, Therese (1808-1878). Viennese-born dancer, known as "la Maestosa" because of her height, took second and supporting place to her sister Franziska, "after the manner of male dancers of the period." (*Grove 3*). She married (morganatically) Prince Adalbert of Prussia and was created Countess von Barnim by the King.

82, 82n8, 85

ERARD. Alsatian family of instrument makers. London and Paris workshops for the manufacture of pianos and harps were founded in the late eighteenth century by Sébastien (1752-1831) and later managed by his nephew Pierre (1796-1855).

20, 21, 26, 27, 32, 34, 35, 44, 67, 68

HÄRTEL, Gottfried Christoph (1763-1827). Director of the Leipzig publishing house Breitkopf & Härtel, and founder of the *Allgemeine musikalische Zeitung*.

94n6

HARVEY, Miss. Unidentified Englishwoman.

76n22, 103

HASLINGER, Tobias (1787-1842). Viennese music publisher. He joined the firm of S.A. Steiner in 1814, and became sole proprietor in 1826. He managed to maintain a high volume and standard of serious publishing by utilizing the profits of printing waltzes by Lanner and Strauss.

18n9, 38n10, 81, 101

HATTON, John Liptrott (1809-1886). Pianist, self-taught composer of popular songs, part-songs, and operettas. Born in Liverpool; settled in London 1832.

75

HAYDN, Franz Joseph (1732-1809)

27n35, 37, 40, 44, 47, 60n55, 82n8, 94 / *Creation*, 76n24 / *Seven Last Words*, 32 / *Symphonies: No. 44*, 104 / *No. 100*, 104 / *No. 102*, 104 / *No. 103*, 104

HÉDOUIN, Pierre (1789-   ?). French lawyer, "littérateur et amateur des arts" (Fétis), bureaucrat, collector, writer of romances (texts).

Romances, 100

HÉROLD, (Louis Joseph) Ferdinand (1791-1833). Parisian composer of operas.

La Clochette, 105 / *Zampa*, 84, 85, 104

HERMANN, J.Z. [Jakob Zeugheer] (1805-1865). Zürich-born violinist, composer, conductor, teacher. He was conductor of the Gentleman's Concerts at Manchester, 1831-1838, and of the Liverpool Philharmonic, 1843-1865.

75

HERZ, Henri (1806-1888). Pianist, composer, and much-sought teacher, Viennese-born but a resident of Paris. Until Liszt's playing consigned him to the wings, Herz was the most celebrated pianist in France. He was a professor at the Conservatoire from 1842 to 1874.

19, 48, 86n17, 89, 89n21, 92n25, 96, 97

HEYSEL, (?). Unidentified German singer.

82n7

HILLER, Ferdinand (1811-1885). German conductor, composer, and teacher of great celebrity; organizer of the Cologne Conservatory; a student and friend of Hummel and a close friend of Mendelssohn for many years.

18, 18n8, 29, 29n40, 30, 32, 34, 101

HIMMEL, Friedrich Heinrich (1765-1814). German piano virtuoso and renowned composer of songs and operas.

Overture, 99

HODGES, C.O. (?- ?). English pianist, possibly the "Mr. Hodges of Bristol" who studied with Hummel at Weimar. A "C. Hodges" is listed as a voice pupil at the Royal Academy of Music, 1827-1829, but did not complete his studies there.

44n26, 54
The music dealer Charles Hodges of Bristol may be related.
39

HOGARTH, George (1783-1870). Scottish-born writer on musical subjects; from 1830, he lived in London, writing for *The Harmonicon* and *The Morning Chronicle*, and was secretary of the Philharmonic Society 1850-1864. He was the son-in-law of George Thomson and the father-in-law of Charles Dickens.

96, 96n11

HORNCASTLE, F.W. (?- ?). Tenor singer, who made numerous appearances at the Philharmonic, 1824-1838, and the Antient Concert, 1833-1846.

73, 74

HORSLEY, William (1774-1858). English organist, composer of glees, sacred music, symphonies, and other instrumental music; a founder of the Philharmonic Society.

55

HOWELL, Thomas. Music dealer in Bristol.

39

HUMMEL, Eduard (1814-1893). Elder son of J.N. Hummel. Pianist, Kapellmeister in Augsburg, Troppau, Brünn, Vienna.

18, 92n26

HUMMEL, Elisabeth Röckel (1793-1883). Opera singer, friend of Beethoven, wife of J.N. Hummel.

9, 18, 29, 81, 81n3, 92

KANDLER, Franz (1792-1831). Austrian music historian, writer and critic for periodicals; staff member and interpreter for Austrian War Office.

102

KEMBLE, Charles (1775-1854). Welsh actor, manager of Covent Garden 1822-1832; a recurrent financial crisis forced his retirement.

75

KIESEWETTER, Christoph Gottfried (1777-1827). German violinist of great celebrity, a resident of London 1821 ff. Fétis felt that London never properly appreciated him, and he died there in great poverty.

54, 55

KLOPSTOCK, Gottlieb Friedrich (1724-1803). German poet.

37

KNOOP, (?) (?-   ?). German (?) cellist, identified by Leipzig *AmZ* as "der Älterer." Active in Meiningen, *ca.* 1837.

89

KNYVETT, Deborah Travis (?-1876). A much sought-after singer for English festivals, especially for Oratorio solos. She was a student of Greatorex and the second wife of William Knyvett.

72, 73, 91n24

KNYVETT, William (1779-1856). The leading male alto in the best London concerts and provincial festivals; a conductor of the Concert of Antient Music from 1832.

72

KÖCKERT, (?) (?-   ?)

82n7, 84

KRAMER, Christian (?-   ?). Clarinetist, music director to the Prince Regent (King George IV). A founding associate of the Philharmonic Society and a member to 1833.

45n28, 54, 55

KREUTZER, Konradin (1780-1849). German composer.

42

LABARRE, Thédor (1805-1870). Parisian composer and harpist, composition student of Fétis and Boieldieu. He made his first tour to England in 1824, and was for some years a successful teacher there.

72

LABLACHE, Luigi (1794-1858). Neapolitan bass, one of Europe's finest singers, known especially for his acting ability. He was of French-Irish descent. First appearance in London: March 30, 1830, in *Il Matrimonio Segreto* (Cimarosa). He was Princess Victoria's singing master, 1836-1837.

63, 72

LAFONT, Charles-Philippe (1781-1839). French violinist, successful in many tours commencing with a prodigy's career. He followed Rode as solo violinist to the Emperor of Russia, and was named first chamber violinist to the King of France and accompanist to the Duchess of Berry.

22 / *Airs suisses,* 22

LAMI, (?) (?- ?). Unidentified French double-bass player.

21, 22, 25n31

LANNEAU, Adolphe de (?- ?)

32n5

LANNEAU, Zima (Mme. Adolphe) de (?- ?)

32

LAPORTE, Pierre François (1799-1841). French comedian, active in London 1824 ff. He was manager of the King's Theatre, 1828-1831, and lessee, actor, and manager at Covent Garden, 1832, but was compelled to retire after suffering heavy losses. From 1833-1841 he was again manager of the King's Theatre. Laporte introduced a great many new Italian operas to London.

79, 80, 83, 84, 85, 86

LEADER. Music dealer in Bath ? [Possibly A. or J.D. Loder?]

39

LEETE, Robert (not later than 1801-1835). English bass singer; conductor of the Glee Club; secretary of the Catch Club; associate of the Philharmonic Society, 1822-1835. His career did not include the major London concert series.

73, 74

LEMOINE, Henri (1786-1854). Eminent Parisian piano teacher and writer of pedagogical works. From 1817 he headed the Lemoine firm of music publishers.

21, 33

MARA, Gertrude Elisabeth (1749-1833). German singer, one of the greatest of the eighteenth century. She was known to have earned a great deal of money several times and to have spent it all.

104

MARCONI-SCHÖNBERGER, (Mme.) Mariane (?- ?). Very low contralto who sometimes sang tenor roles. *Ca.* 1806-1813 she sang at the Italian opera in Vienna (where she probably knew Hummel); in 1819 she is reported in Italy; in the 1820's she was at Stuttgart and Dresden. She also composed.

22, 23

MARIA Paulowna (1786-1859). Russian Grand Duchess of Saxe-Weimar. She was the fifth child of Tsar Paul and Tsarina Maria Feodorowna of Russia, (born Sophia Dorothea Wüttemberg) and married the hereditary Grand Duke Carl Friedrich of Saxe-Weimar.

24n30, 77, 81n3, 82n6

MARSCHNER, Heinrich (1795-1861). German opera composer.

Templer, 84

MASON. Newcastle-under-Lyme music seller.

39

MASON, Monck (?- ?). London theater manager.

79, 80, 85

MASSON, Elizabeth (1806-1865). Popular English soprano. She was a female associate of the Philharmonic Society from 1835 until her death, and a founder of the Royal Society of Female Musicians in 1839.

72, 73, 74

MAYSEDER, Joseph (1789-1863). Viennese violinist and composer. He gave many concerts with Hummel, Moscheles, and Mauro Giuliani, the guitar virtuoso, and was second violinist of Schuppanzigh's string quartet.

17, 36, 41, 41n16

McCOLL, Anna Harrah (?- ?). Alias "Lady of Dunstaffnage." Unidentified Scottish (?) writer and worker for at least one charitable cause.

91, 92n25, 104

MENDELSSOHN, Felix (1809-1847)

18n8, 57n48, 86, 86n17

MERCADANTE, Giuseppe Saverio (1795-1870). Italian opera composer.

Aria, "Se m'abbandoni" (Nitroci), 73

MERIC, Madame de (?- ?). Singer who appeared in London 1832 and 1833. She might be related to Henriette-Clémentine Méric-Lalande (1798-1867), who appeared there in 1830 and 1831 without success, and retired to Spain in 1833.

84, 87

MEYERBEER, Giacomo (1791-1864). German-born composer.

19, 55, 57n48 / *Robert le Diable*, 79

MINORET, Mlle. (?) (?- ?). Unidentified soprano; she sang the lead in *Les Huguenots*, The Hague, 1837.

33n6

MORALT, John Alois (1785-1847). Possibly one of a family of London string players originally from Munich. He was an original member, co-principal, and later principal violist of the Philharmonic, 1831 to 1842, violinist in the Antient Concert, and a busy free-lance player in England.

42, 63, 69

MORI, Nicolas (1796-1839). English violinist, a student of Viotti, for many years a leader of the Philharmonic and other London orchestras including the Antient Concert, and an exceptionally active chamber musician and soloist. Mori, an associate of the Philharmonic from its inception, and a member from 1816, wed the widow of Lewis Lavenu, a music publisher, and became her partner in the business.

49, 53, 63n61, 69, 71, 72

MOSCHELES, Charlotte Embden (1805-1889). Wife of Ignaz Moscheles.

47n35

MOSCHELES, Ignaz (1794-1870). German pianist and composer. He was a student of Dionys Weber, Albrechtsberger, and Salieri; a friend of Clementi, Spohr, Hummel, and Beethoven, for whom he produced a piano score of *Fidelio*. After travelling widely, especially in London and Paris (1820-1825), he married and settled in London, where he became a professor at the Royal Academy of Music and, in 1836, started the "Classical Chamber Concerts," where he performed the music of Scarlatti and Bach on the harpsichord. He also gave London's first piano recitals at a time when such programs were considered truly innovative. In 1846, at Mendelossohn's request, he joined the faculty of the Leipzig conservatory.

18n8, 19, 20, 25n31, 27, 32, 35, 36, 37n8, 39n12, 42, 43, 44, 47, 47n35,

MOSEL, Ignaz Franz Edler von (1772-1844). Viennese civil servant, amateur musician, curator of the Court Library. He was a leader of the anti-Rossini faction in Vienna.

MOUNTAIN, Joseph (?) (?-   ?). Violinist in London, leader at the English Opera House, and co-principal second violin of the Philharmonic, 1819-1840, from which he resigned after the following season. He may be identical with the principal violist of the Antient Concert, 1808-1815. A John Mountain, (1766-   ?) was a member of the Royal Society of Musicians.

MOZART, Wolfgang Amadeus (1756-1791)

MUFF, Joshua. Music dealer in Leeds.

NASS, Frau -(?)- von (?-   ?). Unidentified, possibly the wife of a Breslau violinist mentioned in Leipzig *AmZ* at the time of Hummel's 1828 tour there.

NEATE, Charles (1784-1877). Pianist (student of John Field), and composer (student of Woelfl). He had the friendship and advice of Beethoven for eight months in 1815, and introduced the E-flat piano concerto in England. Neate was one of the original members and a long-time director of the Philharmonic Society.

NEUKOMM, Sigismund Chevalier von (1778-1858). Austro-French composer with a predilection for the style of Palestrina, which he tried to revive. His Requiem for Louis XVI, sung at the Congress of Vienna, earned him the title of Chevalier from Louis XVIII. Neukomm went to London in

1829, and divided the final two decades of his life between there and Paris.

32

NICHOLSON, Charles (1795-1837). English flutist, from 1823 the principal flutist of the opera, Philharmonic, and provincial festivals. He published concerti and solos for the flute as well as a didactic work. See also the note on Böhm.

42, 49, 63

NORBLIN, Louis-Pierre-Martin (1781-1854). Noted cellist in Parisian orchestras and concerts. Cellist at the Théâtre Italien, 1809 ff., and solo cellist at the Opéra, 1811 ff. He was appointed a professor at the Conservatoire in 1826.

21, 22, 23, 25n31

NOVELLO, Vincent (1781-1861). English organist, pianist, composer, editor, and publisher. As organist to the Portuguese Embassy in London he presented the first English performances of Masses by Haydn and Mozart. He helped to organize the Philharmonic Society, and assembled and published many important collections of sacred music.

44, 44n25, 61, 62, 87, 91

NOVELLO & Co. London publishers.

62n59

ONSLOW, (André)-Georges-(Louis) (1784-1853). French-resident composer of an old English noble family. He studied piano with Dussek and Cramer, then turned to the cello. Onslow was well known as a composer of chamber music. He was named an honorary member of London's Philharmonic Society in 1832.

27, 55, 57n48

OTTO, C. (?) (?- ?). Tenor in Leipzig concerts and opera; brother of Franz Otto. He went to London in 1833 as part of a men's part-singing group. See Franz Otto.

87, 88

OTTO, Franz (1809-1842). Bass singer in Leipzig and composer of music for men's choir. He visited London in 1833 as director of a men's part-singing group, in which a brother was a tenor. Their older brother was Ernst Julius Otto, Cantor at Dresden.

87, 88

OURY, Anna Caroline Belleville (1808-1880). Germany's favorite female pianist in the 1820's and 1830's, along with the Leopoldine Blahetka.

She was a student of Czerny. From 1839 to 1866 she and her husband Antonio James Oury resided in London.

19

OURY, Antonio James (1800-1883). English violinist, of Italian noble ancestry; a student of Kreutzer, Baillot, and Lafont. He played in the Philharmonic, 1825-1829, and the Antient Concert orchestra, 1826-1827.

63

PAER, Ferdinando (1771-1839). Italian opera composer. Kapellmeister at the Kärntnerthor Theater, Vienna, 1798 ff., and successor to Spontini as Music Director of the Théâtre des Italiens, Paris, 1812 ff. The Duchess of Berry was his student.

Sargino, 22

PAGANINI, Niccolò (1782-1840). Italian violin virtuoso and composer.

31, 47, 67, 69, 70, 71, 73, 74, 75, 76, 89n21, 104 / *Recitative and variations on three airs,* 73 / *Variations on "Nel cor più,"* 73

PAINE & HOPKINS. London music publisher and dealer.

39

PAISIELLO, Giovanni (1740-1816). Italian opera composer.

37

PALESTRINA, Giovanni Pierluigi da (*ca.* 1525-1594). Italian composer.

32

PANSERON, Auguste Mathieu (1796-1859). Parisian composer, coach at the Opéra Comique, teacher of voice and solfège at the Conservatoire, composer of stage works.

22

PAPENDICK, (?). Unidentified friend of Hummel. One "Papendick," an amateur musician in London, is also mentioned as a friend of the English critic Leigh Hunt.

54

PARRY, John Orlando (1810-1879). Son of the Welsh composer John Parry. He first appeared as Master Parry [Mr. Parry jun.], and was trained as a harpist by Bochsa. Parry later became a comic baritone, but in mature life was best known as an organist and teacher.

72, 75

PASTA, Giuditta (1797-1867). Sensational Italian soprano, known more for her ability to negotiate highly florid lines than for her musicianship. She was most successful in roles by Rossini.

21, 22n23, 59, 72, 87, 88

PATERSON & ROY. Edinburgh music dealer, instrument maker, publisher.

39

PELLEGRINI, Felice (1774-1832). Italian-born bass, for whom Paer wrote the role of the father in *Agnese*. Paris debut: 1819. From 1826 to 1829 he toured in Italy and England, returning then to Paris to become professor of voice at the Conservatoire.

21

PENNY & Son. Music dealer in Sherborne.

39

PETERS, Carl Friedrich (1779-1827). Leipzig music publisher after his purchase of Kühnel's Bureau de Musique in 1814.

18, 18n4, 18n6, 18n10, 29, 94n6, 101

PEUCER, Heinrich Carl (1779-1849). German poet, consistorial director at Weimar.

102

PHILLIPS, Henry (1801-1876). English bass-baritone. Principal bass at the Concert of Antient Music, 1825 ff., and a prominent singer in London's concerts and operas. He sang Caspar in the first English production of *Der Freischütz*, 1824.

49

PIRSCHER, Mme. (?) (?-   ?)

82n7, 83, 84, 85, 87, 88

PIXIS, Johann Peter (1788-1874). German pianist and composer, active in Vienna, 1808-1823 (where he studied with Albrechtsberger), then in Paris, where he settled and was highly successful. He was accompanist for Henriette Sontag's tour of England in 1828.

20, 32, 86n17

PLATT, Henry (1795-1871). English French-horn player. Principal horn, Philharmonic, 1825-1849; Antient Concert, 1827-1848.

42, 63

PLEYEL, Ignace Joseph (1757-1831). Austro-French composer, piano maker, publisher.

21, 33, 38

POTTER, Philip Cipriani Hambly (1792-1871). English pianist, composer, conductor. Professor of piano, Royal Academy of Music; its Principal, 1832-1859; Treasurer of the Royal Society of British Musicians, 1858-1865. He was a student of Attwood, Callcott, and Dr. Crotch.

54

PRESTON, Thomas. London music publisher, music dealer, instrument maker.

39

PURCELL, Henry (1659-1695). English composer.

37

PUZZI, Giovanni (1792-1876). Italian French-horn player, resident in London 1817 ff., and said to be one of the finest horn players of the century. He was soloist with the Philharmonic Society seventeen times, 1817-1837, and appeared at the King's Theatre, Antient Concert, and many festivals and other concerts.

72

RAFFAELLO, Sanzio (1483-1520). Italian painter.

36

RAIMBAUX, Mme. (?) de (?-   ?). Unidentified singer. She appeared at the opera in Naples, 1832 and 1833.

75

RAINER family. Swiss (or Austrian?) entertainers who gave very popular concerts of "Swiss" (Tyrolean?) music (apparently largely yodeling) in the 1820's

50n38

REISSIGER, Karl Gottlieb (1798-1859). German composer and conductor, successor to C.M. von Weber as conductor of the German opera at Dresden.

Libella, 84

RICHARDSON, Moses Aaron. Newcastle book dealer.

39

RICHAULT. Parisian music publishers.

21, 27

RIES, Ferdinand (1784-1838). German pianist, composer, conductor. He was a piano student of, and assistant to, Beethoven, whose musical style greatly influenced his own. Ries lived in London, 1813-1824, and was several times a Director of the Philharmonic Society, membership in which he maintained until his death, even after leaving England. He was later director of the Cäcilia-Verein, Frankfurt.

32, 36, 37, 41, 71 / *Die Räuberbraut,* 79

ROBERTSON, A. Edinburgh music dealer.

39

ROBINSON, John. York music dealer.

39

ROCHEFOUCAULD, Ambroise-Polycarpe de la (1765-1841)

28, **29**

RODE, (Jacques)-Pierre-(Joseph) (1774-1830). French violinist and composer, a student of Viotti. His works are largely violin concerti. After a Paris debut in 1790, he toured in Germany and Russia.

17

RÖCKEL, Josef August (1783-1870). German tenor singer, a professor of voice at the Imperial Opera. In 1829 he boldly undertook the experiment of producing German operas in Paris with a completely German company. His sister was Hummel's wife. Further on this, see p. 79 ff.

79, 79n1, 80, 81, 86, 92, 92n25, 92n26.

ROLLS. Plymouth music dealer.

39

ROMBERG, Andreas Jakob (1767-1821). German violinist and composer, cousin of Bernhard Romberg, cellist and composer.

Symphony No. 1, 102

ROSSINI, Gioacchino Pesaro (1792-1868)

20, 37, 40, 48, 94 / *Cenerentola,* 21, 73, 82n8 / *La Donna del Lago,* 82n8 / *Le Vieux de la Montagne,* 28 / *unidentified quartet,* 22 / *Sigismondo,* 68

RUBINI, Giovanni Battista (1795-1854). Italian tenor. Paris debut: 1825, in *Cenerentola.* The tenor role in Donizetti's *Anna Bolena* was written for him. First London appearance: 1831.

72, 91n24

SABIN. Birmingham music dealer.

39

SCHÜTZE, Johann Stephan (1771-1839). German writer and editor.

101, 103

SALE, John Bernard (1779-1856). English organist, first at St. Margaret's, Westminster; in 1838 he succeeded Thomas Attwood as organist to the Chapel Royal. From *ca.* 1826 he was music instructor to Princess Victoria. He was an associate of the Philharmonic Society in 1816, and member from 1817 to 1855.

71, 73, 74

SALIERI, Antonio (1750-1825). Italian-born composer, especially of operas and cantatas. He was active in Vienna 1766 ff. and helped found the conservatory there. His composition students included Beethoven, Hummel, Liszt, and Schubert.

37

SCHAUROTH, Adolphine (1814-   ?). Pianist, student of Mendelssohn, who dedicated his Piano Concerto Op. 25 to her.

19

SCHIASETTI, Adelaide (?-   ?). Italian mezzo-soprano, also referred to as contralto. She may have been Milanese. In the early 1820's she was singing at the Munich opera; in June, 1824, she was reported leaving for Paris. In the later 1820's she was with the Italian opera in Dresden, in London in 1833, and then in numerous Italian cities. She may have died in 1837.

21, 23

SCHILLER, Johann Christoph Friedrich von (1759-1805). German poet.

37, 87

SCHLESINGER, L. (?-   ?). Unidentified pianist, possibly a pupil of Ries. He performed with the Philharmonic orchestra in 1827 and 1829.

41, 42

SCHLESINGER, Maurice (Moritz) (1798-1871). German-born Parisian music publisher, son of the Berlin publisher Adolf Martin Schlesinger, with whose business his was associated.

20, 21, 27, 33, 101

SCHNEITZHÖFFER, Jean-Madeleine (1785-1852). Parisian composer, mostly of ballets and operas. From 1823 he was director of singing at the Opéra;

from 1833, professor at the choral school of the Conservatoire.

28, 29 / *Sardanapale,* 28

SCHROEDER-DEVRIENT, Wilhelmine (1804-1860). German dramatic soprano. Viennese debut, 1821, as Pamina in *Die Zauberflöte.* She had tremendous successes in *Der Freischütz,* under Weber's direction and *Fidelio,* Vienna, 1822. Her first London appearance: Monck Mason's German opera series, 1832.

84, 85, 88

SCHULTZ, J(ohann?) R(einhold?)

37n8, 39, **39n11,** 44, 54, 55, 99, 100, 101

SCHULZ, Eduard (*ca.* 1814-   ?). Viennese pianist, son of a guitar and harmonica player, S. Schulz. He toured with his brother Leonard (Leonhard).

31, 32n4

SCHULZ, Leonard (Leonhard) (*ca.* 1816-   ?). Viennese guitarist. See Eduard Schulz.

31, 32n4

SCHUMANN, Robert (1810-1856)

95

SCHUNKE, Karl (Charles) (1801-1839). German (?) pianist and composer of salon music. Pianist to the Queen of France.

20, 21, 23

SCRIBE, Augustin Eugène (1791-1861). French dramatist.

28

SEDLATZEK, Jean (?) (1789-   ?). Silesian flute virtuoso, originally trained as a tailor. He established himself in London in 1826.

86

SEIDEL, Maximilian Johann (?-1855). Comic actor, singer in Weimar 1822 ff., later *Regisseur* at the Weimar Court Theater; friend of the Hummels.

81, 82n5, 84, 85, 105

SHIELD, William (1748-1829). English composer of operas, especially for Covent Garden Theatre. Master of the King's Musick, 1817 ff.

The Farmer, 51n39 / *"The Ploughboy,"* 51, 51n39

SINA, Louis (?-   ?). Violinist and violist, possibly French; he may have been living in Vienna, *ca.* 1819.

21

SMART, Sir George Thomas (1776-1867). London organist, vocal teacher, conductor, and occasional composer. He was one of the founders of the Philharmonic Society and conducted forty-nine of its concerts between 1813 and 1844. In 1825 he accompanied Charles Kemble to Germany to engage Weber to compose an opera for Covent Garden; Weber died in Smart's house. He conducted the London premiere of Beethoven's Ninth Symphony (with little success). Sir George was one of the most powerful figures in England's musical world, as a conductor and contractor.

40, 40n14, 15, 46, 46n33, 50, 52, 56n47, 57n48, 57n49, 61, 68, 70, 73n17, 74, 75, 86n17, 87, 89, 89n21, 90n22, 92n26

SONTAG, Henriette, Countess Rossi (1806-1854). One of Europe's greatest sopranos. At the age of seventeen she sang the title role in Weber's *Euryanthe* in Vienna under the composer's direction. In 1824 she was soloist in the first performances of Beethoven's Ninth Symphony and Missa Solemnis. Paris debut: 1826; London debut: 1828. She died in Mexico.

82, 82n7

SONTAG, Nina (?-   ?). Soprano, younger sister of Henriette Sontag. Otherwise unidentified.

82n7, 83, 84, 87, 88

SPAGNOLETTI, P(aolo Diana?) (1768-1834). Italian violinist, resident in England. From 1817, he was leader of the King's Theatre orchestra; Paganini insisted on having him as leader for his London concerts. Spagnoletti appeared under his surname only.

40, 63

SPIEGEL, von und zum Pickelsheim, Baron Karl Emil, Freiherr (1783-1849). Oberhofmarschal at Weimar, Intendant of the Court Theater, Weimar, and as such Hummel's immediate superior.

72, 72n12, 81, 81n3, 83, 84

SPOFFORTH, Reginald (1770-1827). Composer of glees and theatre music. "Hail, smiling morn," from *A Set of Six Glees*, 1799, achieved lasting popularity in England.

"Hail, smiling morn," 73

SPOHR, Louis (1784-1859). German violinist, composer, and conductor active throughout Europe. He was particularly popular in England, as a virtuoso—

he seems to have introduced the conductor's baton to Britain—and later as an oratorio composer.

18n8, 37, 55 / *Jessonda,* 79, 83, 84

SPONTINI, Gasparo (1774-1851). Italian composer; chief Kapellmeister and General Music Director to King Friedrich Wilhelm III at Berlin.

17

STOCKHAUSEN, Franz (1792-1868). Harpist and composer, husband of Margarete Stockhausen.

86

STOCKHAUSEN, Margarete Schmuck (1803-1877). Alsatian concert singer; trained in Paris. She was most successful in England, where she sang almost every year from 1828 to 1840 in Philharmonic, Vocal Society, Benefit, and private concerts. The renowned singer Julius Stockhausen was her son.

45, 49, 57, 59, 62, 67, 68, 70, 72, 86

STREICHER, Johann Andreas (1761-1833). Pianist, teacher, piano manufacturer in Vienna.

61, 61n56

STREICHER, Johann Baptist (1796-1871). Son of the above, who became sole proprietor of the piano firm in 1833.

41n16, 61, 61n56

SZYMANOWSKA, Maria Agata Wolowska (1789-1831). The first internationally famous female Polish pianist. Her style of playing and composing was strongly influenced by Hummel and Field. From 1822 she was Court Pianist to the Tsarina, and moved to St. Petersburg in 1828.

41

TAGLIONI, Marie Sophie (1804-1884). Swedish-born dancer, who was considered the leading member of her profession, although some felt her less versatile than Fanny Elssler. Her activity was centered in Paris. London debut: 1830.

82, 85

TAMBURINI, Antonio (1800-1876). Italian baritone, one of the stars of his epoch, so much so that the non-renewal of his London opera contract in 1840 provoked a series of riots from which his faction emerged victorious. London debut: 1832.

87, 91n24

TERRAIL, J (?). (?- ?). English male alto singer; six Philharmonic appearances 1817-1824; engagements most years at the Antient Concert, 1823-1840, as well as numerous private concerts. Associate of the Philharmonic, 1822-1845.

73, 74

THALBERG, Sigismund (1812-1871). Swiss-born pianist and composer, said to have been a student of Hummel. From 1830-1835 he studied with Pixis and Kalkbrenner in Paris, where he had a sensational success during Liszt's absence in 1836. Liszt's return from Geneva caused intense competition, during which Liszt was supported by Berlioz and Thalberg by Fétis.

91n24

THOMSON, George (1757-1851). Scottish collector and editor of folk songs. He sent the melodies to eminent composers—Haydn, Beethoven, Pleyel, Hummel, and Weber—for the provision of accompaniments.

10n4, 30, 30n2, 43, 43n23, 102, 103, 104.

TITIAN (Tiziano Vecellio) (1477-1576). Italian painter.

36

TULLY, Charles (1785-1845). Britsih French-horn and violin player. Philharmonic fourth, later third horn, 1814-1842; Antient Concerts, likewise, 1829-1843.

40

TULOU, Jean-Louis (1786-1865). French flutist and composer. His career with the Italian and Grand Opera orchestras in Paris was disrupted by the Restoration, because of his firm republican convictions, but he was rehabilitated at the Opéra in 1826 and joined the Conservatory faculty in 1829.

Solo for flute, 21

URHAN, Chrétien (1790-1845). French violinist, violist, organist, composer; a regular violist at Baillot's concerts. He tried to revive the viola d'amore, which he played at Fétis' *Concerts historiques.*

22, 25n31

VAUGHAN, Thomas (1782-1843). English tenor, active in London; Gentleman of the Chapel Royal. In 1813 he became principal tenor of the Antient Concerts, and sang the tenor solo at the Philharmonic's 1825 premier of Beethoven's Ninth Symphony. Associate of the Philharmonic, 1829-1841.

53, 72, 73, 74

WEIGL, Joseph (1766-1846). Austrian composer of operas, of which *Die Schweizerfamilie* was the most popular.

Emmeline, 79 / *Hadrian,* 99 / *Schweizerfamilie,* 79

WEISS, Willoughby Gasper. Liverpool music dealer, partner in (Felix) Yaniewicz and Weiss.

39

WELCH, T. [Thomas Welsh], London music publisher and dealer.

39

WIELAND, Christoph Martin (1733-1813). German poet and writer.

37

WIELE, Adolph (1794-*ca.* 1853). German violinist (student of Baillot) and composer. From 1815-1819, violinist in the Royal Chapel at Stuttgart, where he got to know Hummel. Concert-master at Hesse-Cassel, 1821 ff.

65

WILHELM FRIEDRICH LUDWIG (1797-1888). Prince, later King Wilhelm I of Prussia, later Emperor of Germany.

103

WILLIAM IV (1765-1837). King of England (1830-1837), earlier Duke of Clarence.

64, 73, 74, 76, 81

WILLMAN, Thomas Lindsay (1783-1840). Principal clarinettist in the opera and concert orchestras of London; Master of the Band of the Coldstream Guards.

49, 63, 72

WINTER, Peter von (1754-1825). German composer, especially of operas and sacred music; Court Kapellmeister, Munich, from 1798 until his death.

75

WOOD, Mrs. Mary Anne Paton (1802-1864). Scottish opera and concert soprano (originally a child prodigy violinist). Her second husband was the tenor Joseph Wood. She visited the United States three times in the 1830's, and retired in the 1840's.

91n24

WOOLEY. Nottingham music dealer.

39

WRIGHT, Thomas Henry (1806-1894). English harpist, composer, teacher. His father was Bandmaster of the First Dragoon Guards. Philharmonic appearances, 1833 and 1845.

86, 86n17

ZUCCELLI, Charles (Carlo?) (1792-   ?). Bass singer, born in London to Italian parents. He was engaged at the Théâtre Italien, Paris, 1822-1830, appeared at the Antient Concert in 1822 and 1833, and at the Philharmonic in 1822, 1827-1829, 1833, and 1834.

21, 24